PIANO THEORY FOR BEGINNERS

2 Manuscripts in 1 Book, Including: Music Theory and How to Play Piano

Preston Hoffman

Table of Contents

MUSIC THEORY: FOR BEGINNERS 4
HOW TO PLAY PIANO: IN 1 DAY 92

BOOK 1

MUSIC THEORY: FOR BEGINNERS

The Only 7 Exercises You Need to Learn Music Fundamentals and the Elements of Written Music Today

Preston Hoffman

Table of Contents

Introduction 7
Chapter One: Understanding Music Theory 9
Chapter Two: Learning the Staff 16
Chapter Three: Understanding Common Notation 23
Chapter Four: The Basic Elements Music 39
Chapter Five: Forming Music Scales 45
Chapter Six: Building Intervals 54
Chapter Seven: Key Signatures 61
Chapter Eight: Building Chords 68
Final Words 76
Solutions to Exercise Questions 78

© Copyright 2017 - All rights reserved.

It is not legal to reproduce, duplicate, or transmit any part of this document by either electronic means or in printed format. Recording of this publication is strictly prohibited.

Introduction

Thank you and congratulations on purchasing this book, *"Music Theory: For Beginners"* I have written this book to provide you with the steps that you need to take to understand the fundamentals of music theory from a beginner's standpoint.

One of the most common problems that many people face when it comes to music theory is the inability to get a good book that sticks to the fundamental aspects. Music theory is not exactly a topic that will get your heart pounding, so most people want content that will explain music fundamentals in a clear and concise manner. Most music theory books either bore the reader with long, drawn-out explanations, or they toss in some complex concepts that leave you totally confused.

However, this is where this book is different. This book provides you with the only seven exercises that you need as a beginner to master the fundamental elements of written music. These interactive exercises are all based on seven topics that form the basis of every good music theory course. The exercises are spread throughout the book so that once you finish reading each chapter, you can test yourself. I have taken the time to make the questions as challenging as possible yet simple enough for any beginner to understand. In any case, the answers have been provided at the end of the book.

You will not find yourself struggling with complex theories here. I have written this book with the beginner in mind, so every chapter covers a single aspect of music theory. This is to ensure that you move step-by-step, mastering one foundational topic before you move onto the next one. You will learn the common notation system, scales, clefs, key signatures, intervals, chords, and much more.

I have tried to make sure that the topics move sequentially in terms of the level of difficulty. My goal is to take your hand and walk you through every topic and exercise so that you feel comfortable with the content. From my experience with reading and writing music, I know that if you get the first step right, then the next one will automatically fall into place.

By the time you finish reading this book, you will be much more confident in reading and even writing your own music. Yes, it's true! The exercises you will go through in this book will test you and help you grow your musical abilities. I can promise you that with this book, you will finally get to learn all you ever wanted to know about music theory in a fun and interactive way. This is a personal guarantee!

Are you ready? Let's go!

Chapter One: Understanding Music Theory

In this chapter, you will learn about what music theory is all about and why it is important for beginners to have a firm theoretical foundation. You will also go through a brief and painless history of written music. Finally, you will get to discover the seven exercises that are fundamental to the learning of music.

What is Music Theory?

The simplest way to define music theory is this: It is the language that enables you to read, understand, and play any kind of music that has been composed. Music theory is made up of rules and concepts that are designed to govern the way music is written and performed.

Another way to look at it is that music is a language that consists of many various parts. Each part is then divided into smaller sections. If you want to learn how to speak the whole language, you must start by learning the smaller sections first and how to combine them to form the larger parts. Then you must learn how to put together those large parts to communicate whatever message you have through that language.

We learn music theory so that we know how to put the elements together to compose music. That is music theory in a nutshell.

As a beginner, it is easy to fall into the trap of feeling overwhelmed when you hear the words "music theory," but there is really nothing to worry about. The critical thing to keep in mind when learning about music theory is that the music preceded the theory. The art of making musical sounds dates back thousands of years, and at that time, our ancestors didn't have any kind of theory to rely on. They just pounded on their drums and played it by ear. If you are already playing an instrument, then you most likely have a rough idea about music theory. The only issue is that you haven't learned the terms and technicalities yet.

Like I said before, music theory is a language that allows musicians to read and perform compositions the way the composer intended. However, it is important to also note that there are some musicians who are not able to read or write music, yet they can still make awesome melodies and sounds. There are some people who can hear and speak English but cannot read or write it. Therefore, some people view learning music theory as boring and unnecessary.

On the other hand, I believe that a student can progress much further in learning a new language by training himself/herself to read and write it. It is the same with music theory. If you want to master new techniques, gain more confidence, and perform new styles, you need to learn music theory.

Now let's go back a bit into history to unearth the beginnings of music theory.

Musical Beginnings

According to historians, complex musical instruments were already being used as far back as 7000 B.C. Archaeologists have found bone flutes that can still be used to create short performances for modern listeners to hear.

There are pictographs from 3500 B.C. that depict the ancient Egyptians playing clarinets, harps, and lyres. By the year 1500 B.C., the people in Northern Syria had modified the Egyptian harp and created the first ever two-stringed guitar. The instrument even had tuning pegs and a hollow soundboard for amplifying sounds.

So why am I telling you all this?

If you look at the history of ancient music, you will realize that distinct cultures spread out all over the world were able to create music with very similar tonal qualities. How was this possible? It is believed that certain patterns of musical notes just sound right while others do not. If this is the case, then music theory is simply the search for why and how certain notes sound right or wrong. To put it more plainly, music theory is important because it helps us understand *why* an object sounds a particular way and *how* we can reproduce that exact sound.

Ancient Greece is believed to be the origin of music theory. The Greeks even built schools that taught the science and philosophy of analysing music. It was Pythagoras who went as far as creating the 12-pitch octave scale that resembles the one we currently use today. Pythagoras achieved this using a device known as the Circle of Fifths, which you will learn about later in this book.

A lot of the musical theory you are about to learn is based on the works of the ancient Greeks. But unlike the Greek language, this book is much simpler to read and understand.

The Significance of Theory in Your Music

It is easy to think that making great music is as simple as sitting down, playing whatever note you want, going in any direction you see fit, and even stopping at any stage of the performance. That is often the view of most aspiring musicians who would love to play an instrument.

However, such kind of performances, if they do exist, would cause confusion and sound annoying to the listeners. Only those musicians who have thoroughly mastered how to stack notes and chords adjacent to each other can manage to perform a spontaneous jam that listeners would love. In other words, since music is a language that communicates a message, you must learn how to connect with your listeners at all times.

Learning musical theory can also inspire you a great deal, as you will soon find out after you finish reading this book. It is a tremendously great feeling when you discover that you can put together a chord progression and create an awesome song out of it. How would you feel if you could look at a piece of classical music and know that you can play it for the first time?

What about being confident enough to call up your friends and ask them to come over and jam with you? You wouldn't be able to do that without learning music theory since you need a way to communicate with other musicians. You use music theory to talk to one another as you play your various instruments.

The truth is that music theory will broaden your horizons as a musician. If you see yourself as a potential rock guitarist, you will be able to know which notes to play in which key. If it's classical music you are interested in, you will know how to sight-read and maintain a consistent beat. Music is fun but it also requires a prominent level of discipline. At the end of it all, it is worth it!

The Seven Fundamental Exercises

There are a lot of elements that you will have to learn to become an accomplished musician. Of course, we all wish that we could somehow sit down with an instrument and start playing beautiful music without going through the hassle of any formal training. But the reality is that you need structured exercises that will prepare you for your future as a music maestro.

In the next few chapters, we are going to cover music theory fundamentals that will help you get started. There are seven elements that you will have to master to learn these elements effectively. They are:

1. Learning the staff and music alphabet
2. Common notation
3. Basic elements of music (rhythm, melody, harmony, etc)
4. Mastering the scales
5. Building intervals
6. Understanding key signatures
7. Forming chords

Every single one of these elements is critical to your progress as a beginner. They will teach you the individual elements of music and how they are put together to create a solid foundation for reading, playing, and studying music.

Chapter Summary

Here is a summary of the key points of this chapter:

- Music theory is the rules and concepts that enable us to read, understand, and play any kind of musical composition.
- It is possible to play music without learning music theory, but if you want to go further in learning new techniques and performing new styles, you must learn music theory.
- Though complex musical instruments date back as far as 7000 B.C., the ancient Greeks are the ones credited with establishing schools for analysing the elements of music.
- Learning musical theory will enable you to communicate more effectively with listeners and fellow musicians, while also inspiring confidence in your own musical abilities.
- There are seven key exercises that will help you learn the fundamentals of music theory.

In the next chapter, you will learn about the staff and how we use the music alphabet to write music. It isn't a difficult topic, but since the rest of the book will be based on what you learn in the next chapter, you need to make sure that you go through it thoroughly.

Chapter Two: Learning the Staff

In this chapter, you will learn about the staff. It is important to start by learning the main way that we write music. You will learn what the staff looks like, the several types of clefs, and how to arrange notes when writing your music. There will also an exercise at the end of the chapter to test what you have learned.

Human beings started making music way before writing was invented. Even to this day, some musicians choose to play "by ear," which means they don't rely on written music. However, it is important to write music so that it can be shared and studied. This means that we must have system to represent music, hence the need for a music alphabet.

What is the Music Alphabet?

The musical alphabet is an arrangement of letters that enables us to write the sounds that we want to play. Every time you sit down to play music with others, the first thing you do is talk about what you plan on playing. By talking I don't mean just telling each other stories or describing your music verbally. The language of communication should be specific to music, and that is where the music alphabet comes in. The alphabet is the means of representing your music.

Before we go into the musical notes themselves, let's start by learning about the most widespread way of writing music. This is the staff.

The Staff

Now that you have learned about the music alphabet, it's time to tackle a very important component of music. All instruments that play specific pitches are written on the staff, which is comprised of five horizontal parallel lines. Music notes are usually placed either on the lines or in the spaces between the lines. The music on a staff is read from left to right.

In the image below, you will notice some short lines that are above or below the staff. These are known as ***ledger lines***. These are used to show a note that is too low or too high to be placed on the staff.

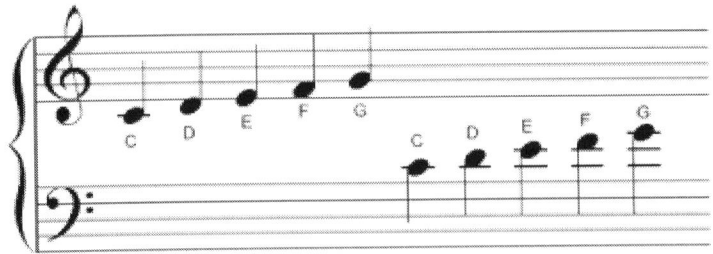

Figure 2.1

To make reading music much easier, vertical lines are used to split the staff into sections. These lines are known as **_bar lines_**. Each section that is formed on the staff is then called a **_measure_** or **_bar_**. At the end of every staff, there are two lines that mark the end of a section of music or song. These are known as **_double bar lines_**. A heavy double bar line indicates that you have reached the end of the song. A light double bar line means the end of a section of music.

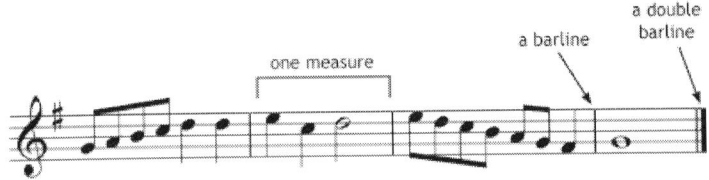

Figure 2.2

You may be wondering what some of the symbols and shapes are on the staff above. These will be discussed later in this chapter.

Clefs

In figure 2.2, you notice a symbol that is placed at the beginning of the staff. This is the ***Clef symbol***. It tells you the type of note that is found on every line and space of the staff. There are two kinds of clefs; the treble clef (or G clef) and the bass clef (or F clef).

The reason why it's called a G clef is that its body curls around the line that represents the G note. For the F clef, the symbol curls around the line representing the F note. The notes in the staff are always arranged in ascending order from top to bottom, but they are positioned differently depending on the type of clef being used. The reason why we use different clefs is to cover as many notes within the human voice range as possible, as well as most of the instruments used. People and instruments with high voice ranges use the treble clef while those with lower ranges use bass clef.

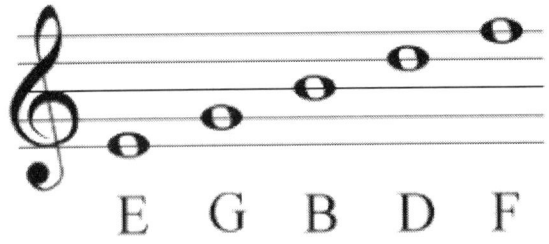

Figure 2.3

Figure 2.4

Exercise 1

1. Draw the staff on a piece of paper and practice writing the two clef symbols on the staff. Draw as many as you can until you learn it perfectly.

2. Draw the staff with treble and name all the spaces on the staff.

3. Draw the staff with bass clef and name the lines in it.

4. On a staff with a treble clef, name the ledger lines and spaces above the staff.

5. On a staff with a bass clef, name the lines and spaces below the staff.

Chapter Summary

Here are some key points you need to remember:

- The musical alphabet is an arrangement of letters that enable us to write the sounds that we want to play.
- The notes on the staff are placed either on the lines or in the spaces between the lines.
- Notes on the staff are arranged in ascending order.
- Ledger lines are used when showing notes that are too high or too low to appear on the staff.
- A bar line splits the staff into sections called measures or bars.
- A heavy double bar line indicates the end of a song.
- A light double bar line indicates the end of a section of music.

- There are two types of clef symbols – the treble clef and the bass clef.

In the next chapter, you will learn about music notation. These are considered the building blocks of music and are necessary when writing your music.

Chapter Three: Understanding Common Notation

In this chapter, you will learn the A-B-C's of the musical language. We will talk about the building blocks that form the foundation of musical theory. These include notes, pitch, octave, beats, and time signature. There will also an exercise at the end of the chapter to test what you have learned.

Common notation simply refers to the standard system that we use to represent music notes. It is more widely used than other types of music notation that have been invented, for example, tablature. You have already learned about one part of common notation in the previous chapter. Now let's talk about notes and pitches.

Notes

Every piece of music you will encounter consists of notes. They are the building blocks of music. A note is simply a letter of the musical alphabet that represents the ***pitch*** made by a musical instrument.

The pitch of a note refers to how low or high it sounds. Pitch is dependent on the frequency and wavelength of the sound wave of a note. If the frequency of the sound wave is high, and the wavelength is short, the pitch will be high. Since very few musicians are keen on such kind of physics terminologies, they use letters to represent different pitches.

There are seven letters that form the music alphabet. These are:

A B C D E F G A

or:

C D E F G A B C

These seven letters are used to name the white keys on a keyboard. As you can see above, you start with the letter A and proceed to the letter G. After G, instead of going to H, we go back and start counting from A. In music, each set of seven letters (A – G or C - B) is referred to as an *octave*. The moment you reach the eighth note, you begin the next octave.

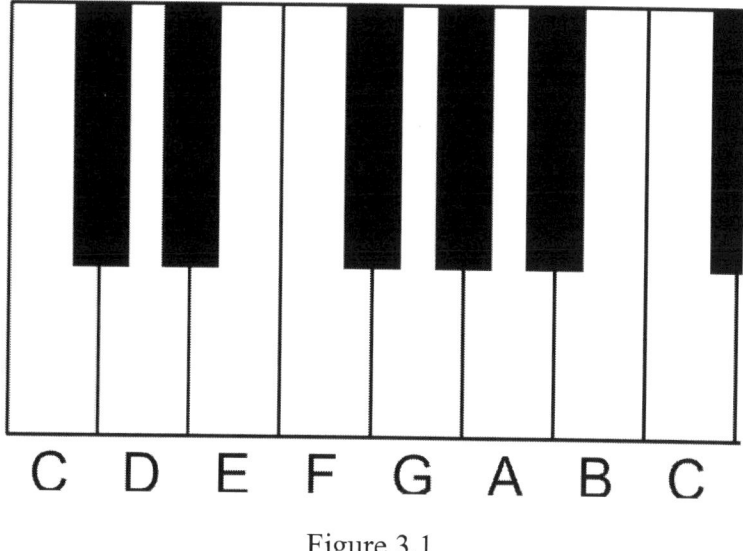

Figure 3.1

But there's one thing that you need to be keenly aware of here. As you move toward the right side, or *up the alphabet*, you realize that you will meet a note with the same letter name as another one before. However, this next note will be at a higher octave than the previous one.

In figure 3.1 above, the second C note has a pitch that is at a higher octave than the first. If you were to move up the alphabet, the third C note would be a higher pitch than the second one, and so on. You can also move in the opposite direction, and this is referred to as going *down the alphabet*.

Sharps and Flats

Though there are only seven letters in the music alphabet, there are more than seven notes. The seven letters from A to G represent *natural* notes. Natural simply means it is a regular note. However, there are five other notes that are usually placed in-between these natural notes. This brings the total number of notes in the music alphabet to 12. These five other notes are represented as **sharp notes** (♯) and *flat notes* (♭).

A sharp note is a note that is higher in pitch than its natural letter. For example, G♯ (pronounced G sharp) is higher than G. On the other hand, a flat note is a note lower than its natural letter, so A♭ (pronounced A flat) is lower in pitch than A. These sharp and flat notes are used to represent the black keys on a keyboard.

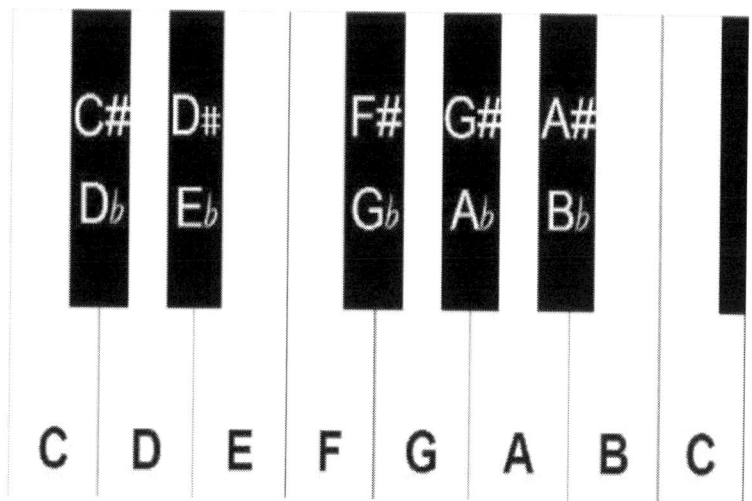

Figure 3.2

From the image above, you can see that in some instances, the sharps and flats occupy the same key. This means that they refer to the same note but are given different names depending on where they are used. This is what is known as **enharmonics**. In other words, F♯ is the same note as G♭, and C♯ is the same note as D♭, and so on.

If you are keen, you may have noticed that there are some notes that do not have any sharps or flats between them. This happens between the E-F notes and B-C notes. This shouldn't be taken to mean that there is no E♯ or C♭. We simply refer to them as F or B. So, when you raise an E by one note you get an F. Also, when you lower a C note you get a B.

The sharp symbol usually indicates that the particular note is one half-step higher than its natural equivalent. For example, G♯ is one half-step higher than G. In the same way, the flat symbol indicates that the note is one half-step lower than its natural equivalent. So, A♭ is one half-step lower than A.

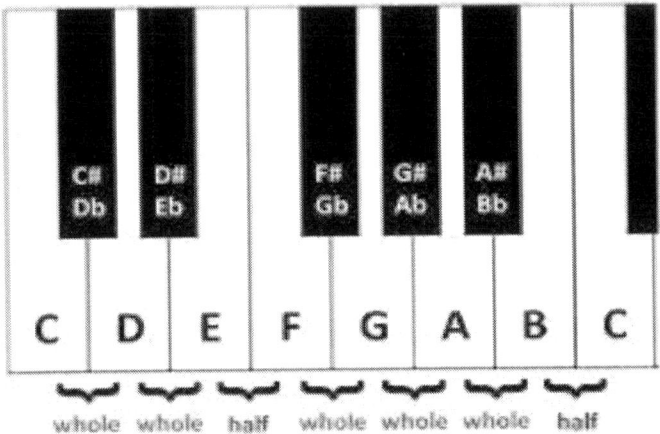

Figure 3.3

In other words, the distance between the G note and the A note is *one whole step*. When you see two adjacent notes having a sharp or a flat note between them, then that means that they are a whole step apart. Therefore, from figure 3.3, it is clear to see that most of the notes on the keyboard are one whole step apart except the E-F notes and B-C notes. These are only one half-step apart.

Parts of a Note

In common notation, sounds are written in form of notes. The two most critical pieces of information that written music should convey to a musician are the pitch to be played and its duration. A note that is placed high on the staff should be played at a higher sound.

To determine the pitch of a note, look at the clef, key signature, and the line or space the note is placed. To determine the duration of a note (how long it lasts), you look at the shape of the note, its tempo, and time signature.

There are three specific parts of a note. There is the head, the stem, and the flag.

- **The Head** (3) – This is the rounded section of a note. The head can be shaded or hollow. Every note must have a head.

- **The Stem** (2) – This is the vertical straight line that is linked to the head. Quavers, crotchets and minims all contain stems. Stems can point either up or down depending on the position of the note on the staff. Notes on or above the centre line have stems pointing down. Notes below the centre line have stems pointing up.

- **The Flag** (1) – This is the line that sticks out from the top or bottom of the stem. Only quavers and shorter notes carry flags.

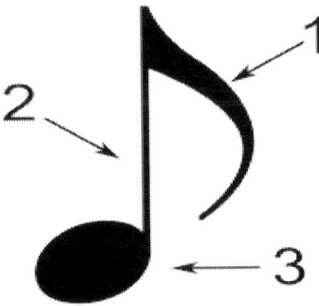

Figure 3.4

The pitch of a note is determined by the position of the head of the note, not the entire body. The head, the stem and the flag are all factors that must be considered when deciding how much time a note is given.

Note Duration and Values

Note duration is defined as the amount of time that a note is played. Each note usually has its own value, and these include the semibreve, minim, crotchet, quaver, and semiquaver. They are shown in this exact order in the image below.

Figure 3.5

The Whole (Semibreve) Note

This note is represented by a hollow oval and has no stem. It is the longest note in modern music and lasts for a full four beats.

This means that for four entire beats, all you must do is play and hold that one note.

The Half (Minim) Note

This is half the value of a semibreve and is held for half as long as the whole note. Two minims occupy the same length of time as a semibreve. It is represented by a hollow oval with a stem.

The Quarter (Crotchet) Note

This is a quarter of a semibreve. Four crotchets occupy the same length of time as a semibreve, which means a crotchet is one beat long. It is represented by a shaded oval with a stem.

The Eighth (Quaver) Note

This is half the length of time as a crotchet. It is represented by a shaded oval with a stem and a flag. The flag cuts the value of a note by half.

The Sixteenth (Semiquaver) Note

Two semiquavers occupy the same length of time as one quaver. It is represented by a shaded oval with a stem and two flags.

If two notes that have flags are next to each other, they are sometimes connected using a ***beam***. This makes it possible to group flagged notes so that the music is easier and faster to read. The same principle also applies to semiquavers. A note must have the same number of beams as it does flags.

Figure 3.6: Semiquaver with beam

Dotted Notes

By now you know that a minim is half the length of a semibreve; a crotchet is half of a minim, and so on. But what do you do if you want a note length that is not half of another note? That's where the dotted note comes in. A dotted note is 1 ½ times the length of the same note. So, you end up with the original note length and half of that note length. For example, a dotted minim would have a duration that is as long as a minim plus a crotchet; or three crotchets.

If a note has two dots, it simply means that each dot adds half the length of the previous note. This is shown in figure 3.7 below.

𝅗𝅥. = 𝅗𝅥 + 𝅘𝅥

𝅘𝅥. = 𝅘𝅥 + 𝅘𝅥𝅮

𝅘𝅥.. = 𝅘𝅥 + 𝅘𝅥𝅮 + 𝅘𝅥𝅯

Figure 3.7

Time Signatures

These are usually indicated at the front end of the staff and are placed after the clef symbol and key signature. The time signature doesn't appear on every staff. It is used only when there is a change in the meter. *Meter* refers to the basic rhythm of the music. Time signature represents the meter and tells you how you should write it.

A fraction represents time signatures. The number at the top indicates the number of beats per measure while the number at the bottom indicates the type of note that will be used to carry the beat. The next section explains this more clearly.

Figure 3.7

Beats

There are many ways to organize music, and one of them is by splitting the time into small periods known as ***beats***. Most of the actions that go with a piece of music occur at the start of the beat. For example, when you tap your foot or clap your hands, you are making those sounds or movements at the start of the beat. This is usually referred to as being "on the downbeat" since it corresponds to the moment when the conductor's baton reaches the bottom of its path.

The downbeat is the most substantial section of a beat, though some are stronger than the rest. Beats form a pattern such as strong-weak-weak-strong-weak-weak. Therefore, beats are further grouped into measures or bars. For example, a beat such as strong-weak-weak-strong-weak-weak would be written as 1-2-3-1-2-3, which means that each measure must contain three beats.

We already talked about how time signature indicates the number of beats per measure and the kind of note that carries a beat. For example, figure 3.7 has a time signature that requires three quarter (crotchet) notes in all the measures on that particular staff. In other words, every measure will have three crotchets. We usually say that such a piece is in "three four" time.

Don't forget what we learned earlier. A crotchet (quarter) note is one beat long. In other words, every measure on the staff should have the equivalent of three beats. These can still be represented as one minim and a crotchet, or six quavers per measure.

Exercise 2

1. Complete the following series of natural notes: A B _ _ E F _ _

2. Provide an alternative name for the following:

    a. A♯

    b. D♭

    c. G♭

    d. E♭

Fill in the blanks:

3. 1 semibreve = _____ quavers

4. 1 minim = _____ quarters

5. 1 minim = 1 quarter + _____ eighths

6. Draw two staves with a treble clef symbol and time signatures showing *two four-time, three eight time,* and *six four time*. Fill in each measure with a different combination of note lengths. Use at least one dotted note in each staff.

Chapter Summary

Here are some of the key points you need to remember:

- A note is a letter that represents the pitch made by a musical instrument.
- An octave is a set of notes from one letter to the next pitch by the same letter name.
- The symbol ♯ represents sharp notes.
- Flat notes are represented by the symbol ♭.
- Enharmonics are two notes that have equal pitches but are known by different names.
- There are five note values - semibreve, minim, quarter, quaver, and semiquaver. Each note lasts half the beat of the previous one.
- Music is divided into short time periods called beats.
- The time signature is shown using a fraction. The number at the top indicates the number of beats per measure. The number at the bottom indicates the type of note that will be used to carry the beat.

In the next chapter, you will learn about the building blocks of music. These are the basic elements of every musical piece, and they include aspects like rhythm, harmony, melody, timbre, and dynamics.

Chapter Four: The Basic Elements Music

In this chapter, you will learn about the essential elements that make music what it really is. These are aspects that even non-musicians can understand. As long as you have an appreciation for good music, you should be able to pick out these musical building blocks.

We are going to cover a number of these basic elements here. It is also important to note that musical theory experts hold differing opinions as to the total number of the elements of music. Some claim that there are as few as four while others say that there are as many as 10. Here we shall be covering rhythm, harmony, melody, timbre, texture, and dynamics.

Creating Rhythm

The primary reason why we study music theory is to be able to describe different musical pieces regarding how similar or different they are about the above six elements. Rhythm is considered one of the most basic components of any kind of music. Some types of music don't have harmony or melody, but every piece of music must have rhythm.

So, what exactly is rhythm?

Rhythm can be defined as the pattern of sounds repeated throughout the music. We can also say that rhythm is the arrangement of note lengths in music. Music and time go hand in hand, which means that rhythm has to be heard over a period of time. Rhythm is usually shaped by the meter and incorporates other elements such as *tempo* and *beat*.

Tempo is the speed at which you play a particular piece of music. When creating a composition, you indicate the tempo using an Italian word. For example, if you look at the starting point of a score, you may see words like *Largo* (slow pace), *Moderato* (moderate pace), or *Presto* (very fast pace). Here are some common tempo markings and their translations:

- Adagio – slow
- Vivo – lively and brisk
- Lento – slow
- Molto – a lot
- Mosso – motion or movement
- Piu – more
- Allegro – fast
- (un) poco – a little
- Meno – less

Harmony

Harmony is the result of having more than one pitch being heard at the same time. When you hear two or more notes being played at one time, you are listening to harmony. Harmony provides support for the melody and gives it texture. Harmony is usually described as being diminished, augmented, major, and minor.

Melody

Melody can be described as the general tune that is created when you play a succession of notes. It is influenced by your rhythm and pitch. A musical piece can have just one melody running through it, or it may have several melodies stacked in a verse-chorus form.

Timbre

Timbre is the quality of a sound that differentiates one musical instrument or voice from another. It is also called *tone color*. Timbre has nothing to do with the volume, length, or pitch of a sound.

For example, if you play a specific note on a clarinet and then on an oboe for five seconds at a specific volume, a listener can easily know that the notes are different. This is because the timbre of a clarinet is different from that of an oboe.

Texture

This refers to the type and number of layers that are used in a musical composition. Texture can be a single melodic line (monophonic), several melodic lines (polyphonic), or the main melody together with chords (homophonic).

Dynamics

This is the intensity that a musical piece is performed. In written music, dynamics are represented by symbols or abbreviations that indicate the volume that a note should be sung or played. Just like tempo, dynamics are derived from Italian words. For example, *fortissimo* indicates an extremely loud passage while *pianissimo* indicates an extremely soft section of music.

Here are some typical dynamic markings:

- mf mezzo forte   = medium loud

- f   forte   = loud
- ff fortissimo   = very loud
- fff fortississimo   = very, very loud
- p   piano   = soft
- pp pianissimo   = very soft
- mp mezzo piano   = medium soft

Exercise 3

1. Test yourself and see whether you can interpret what these Italian tempo markings mean:
   - Poco pin mosso
   - Piu vivo
   - Un poco allegro
   - Molto adagio

2. Write these dynamics in order from the quietest to the loudest: f, p, mf, ff, pp, and mp

Chapter Summary

Here are some of the key points you need to remember:

- Rhythm is the pattern of sounds repeated throughout the music.
- Rhythm depends on the tempo and beat of the music
- Tempo refers to the pace of the music and is usually indicated by Italian words.
- Harmony is created when more than one pitch is played at the same time.
- Melody is the general tune created when a succession of notes is played. A musical piece can have one or more melodies.
- Timbre is what tells us the difference between sounds made by different instruments.
- Texture is the number and type of layers in a musical composition. It can be monophonic, polyphonic, or homophonic.
- Dynamics is the intensity that music is played, and its markings are derived from Italian words.

In the next chapter, you will learn more about the different types of music scales. These are considered to be subsets of the notes you learned in Chapter 3.

Chapter Five: Forming Music Scales

In this chapter, you will learn how to create the different types of music scales. You will start with the simplest one, which is the major scale, and then proceed onto the more complex minor scale.

Music scales can be described as a set of notes arranged in sequential order, chosen to be used for a particular song. Why do we choose those notes? Simply because they sound great together! Though different cultures have adopted a variety of scales, the most common one is the major scale.

In order to create a scale, you need to go through the music alphabet (remember the seven letters from A to G?) and pick out notes that go well together. The notes chosen must achieve a particular sound. In most cases, you can do this by combining whole steps and half steps.

Tonal Centre

Every scale begins with the note that it is named after. That particular note is referred to as the ***tonal centre*** of that scale, and it is where the music in that scale feels "at rest."

For example, in most cases, music in the C major scale always ends on a C major chord. The music will begin on the C note, return to the C note repeatedly, and the melody will be based on the C note so much that listeners be able to identify where the tonal centre of that piece of music is.

Major Scales

If you have ever heard a song that sounds cheerful, uplifting, and fun, then it was probably written in a major key. Music that is written using a particular key only uses some of the many notes available. This sequence of notes then forms what we call a scale. Major keys are used to build major chords to then form a major scale.

It is important to know that different songs can use different scales, and different parts of a song can also make use of different scales. Scales are normally written in a sequential order from one note to the next note of the same letter. For example, we can have a scale that ranges from note C to the next note C, as shown below.

C D E F G A B C

As we already learned, each set of seven letters of the music alphabet forms an octave. Therefore, we can say that the above scale is a one-octave scale. To create a two-octave scale, you simply continue the same sequence until you land on the next note with the same letter name.

C D E F G A B C D E F G A B C

The range of notes from C to C is what forms the scale for C major. None of the notes in this particular scale has a sharp or a flat. On the other hand, the D major scale has two sharps. These are F sharp and C sharp.

D E F♯ G A B C♯ D

So, the question you are probably asking is: How are we supposed to know which notes should be sharpened and which ones should be flattened? The first method involves the use of a chart. However, this can be a cumbersome way since you have to keep referring all the time. You may even be forced to cram all that information into your head. The better alternative is to learn how to use whole and half steps.

Whole Steps and Half Steps

We talked about how the pitch of a sound represents how high or low the sound is. In music, we usually say that one note is either much higher or lower than another. This distance between two pitches is known as a half step. If you look at figure 5.1 below, you will be able to understand this better. This method of counting up whole and half steps can be used to form music scales from scratch.

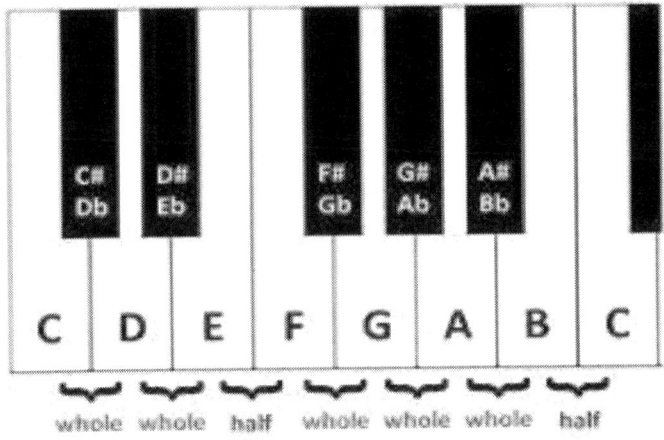

Figure 5.1

For example, we know that the distance from A to A♯ is a half step. The distance between B and B♭ is a half step. In other words, two consecutive half steps form a whole step. The format of any major scale usually follows this kind of sequence:

whole whole half whole whole whole half

This can also be written as:

w w h w w w h

This sequence means that there is a whole step between the first and second note, the second and third note, the fourth and fifth note, the fifth and sixth note, and the sixth and seventh note. There is a half step between the third and fourth note and the seventh and eighth note.

Please memorize this pattern because every major scale you encounter from here onwards will use this same sequence.

So, if we want to form the C major scale, we can write it as:

C w D w E h F w G w A w B h C

Figure 5.2

However, if we want to form the D major scale, we can write it as:

D w E w F♯ h G w A w B w C♯ h D

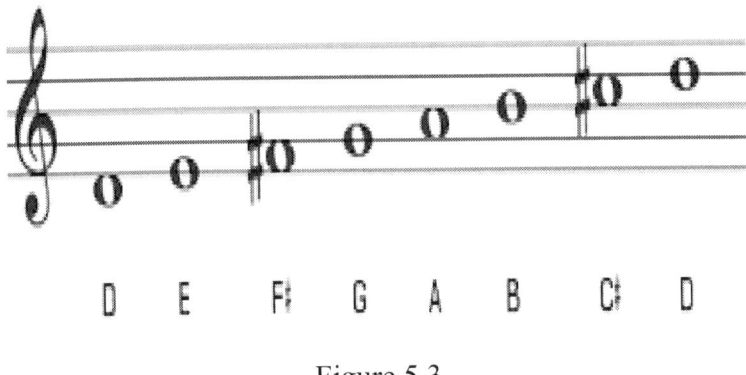

Figure 5.3

Minor Scales

Most people think of minor scales as confusing. This is because many music students usually start learning about the major scale first and end up focusing on it more than the minor scale. This situation isn't helped by the fact that there are a number of different types of minor scales that are often confused with one another. However, we will only focus on the most common minor scale in this book.

It is important to note that a piece of music in a particular major scale will sound the same as music in another major scale. For example, music that is in C major will sound somewhat similar to music in D major.

However, music in D major will sound very different from that in D minor because the notes in a minor scale are arranged in a very different pattern. Music written using a minor key has a sad, ominous, or mysterious sound than that written using a major key.

Natural Minor Scale

A natural minor scale is a scale where every note is played in a minor key signature. A natural minor scale is formed by starting at the tonal centre and moving upward using the following step pattern:

Whole half whole whole half whole whole

w h w w h w w

For example, music written in D minor scale will look like this:

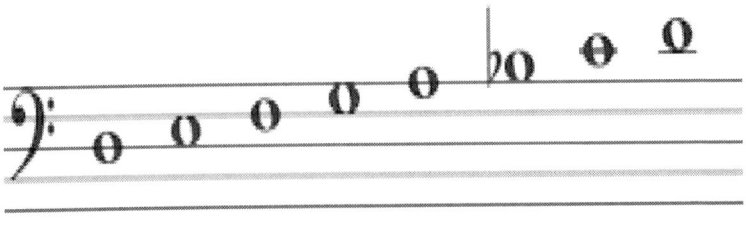

D E F G A B♭ C D

Figure 5.4

Exercise 4

1. Draw a staff with a treble clef. Write down the notes of the A major scale.

2. Draw a staff with a bass clef. Write down the notes of the G flat major scale.

3. Draw a staff with a treble clef. Write down the notes of the F minor scale.

4. Draw a staff with a treble clef. Write down the notes of the A flat minor scale.

Chapter Summary

Here are the key points to remember from this chapter:

- A music scale is a set of notes that sound good together, arranged in sequential order, within a particular piece of music.
- The tonal centre is the first note in a scale and is used to name that particular scale.
- To remember the sequence of notes in a major scale, follow the pattern *w w h w w w h*.
- A natural minor scale is written in a minor key and follows the pattern *w h w w h w w*.

In the next chapter, you will learn about the different types of intervals and how they are built.

Chapter Six: Building Intervals

In this chapter, you will learn about the different types of intervals and how to name them. Intervals are a very important concept in music. In fact, you cannot learn about scales or chords without making some reference to intervals. As a serious student of music theory, you must take the time to learn intervals and how to identify them.

Defining Intervals

An interval can be defined as the distance or space between two notes or pitches. Intervals are described using whole steps and half steps, which we have already covered in the previous chapters. The uncomplicated way to describe an interval would be to say, "E natural is one-half step below F natural," or "A flat is one step and a half away from F."

However, these are small distances. What about when we need to describe longer intervals in a major or minor scale?

How to Name Intervals

The primary factor you have to consider when naming an interval is the distance between the two notes. You need to look at how the notes are presented and then count the spaces and lines between the notes in the staff. Make sure that you include the spaces or lines that the notes are positioned on.

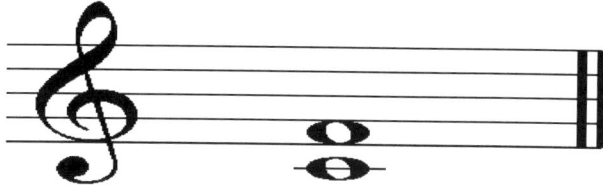

Figure 6.1

Figure 6.2

In figure 6.1 above, the interval between the C and F notes is four. We refer to this *a fourth*. In figure 6.2, the interval count between C and E is a third. At this point, the type of clef, key signature, and accidental (flats and sharps) don't matter.

If the interval between the notes is less or equal to one octave, it is referred to as a **simple interval** *(fig 6.3)*. If the interval is greater than one octave, it is called a **compound interval** *(fig 6.4)*.

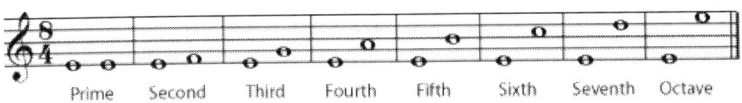

Figure 6.3

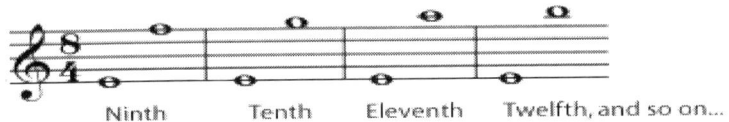

Figure 6.4

Now in the next phase of identifying an interval, we will consider the clef, key signature, and accidentals.

Perfect Intervals

Certain intervals are considered to be perfect intervals. They include primes, fourths, fifths, and octaves. They are called perfect because their sound waves are related very closely to one another. This makes these intervals sound good together.

Another name for a perfect prime is **unison,** which represents two notes that produce the same pitch. A perfect fourth has 5 half steps and a perfect fifth has 7 half steps. A perfect octave is where two notes are eight intervals apart, that is, 12 half steps apart. It is important that you understand how these steps are counted. You can go back and refresh your knowledge from the previous chapter on scales.

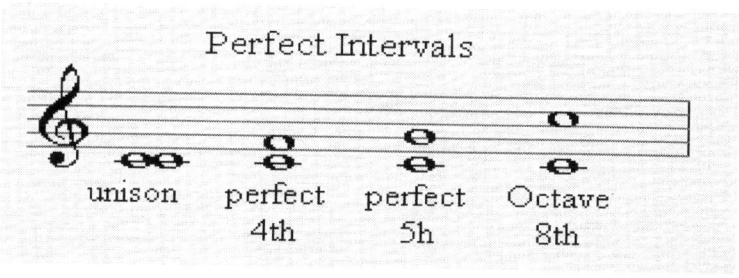

Figure 6.5

Major and Minor Intervals

The rest of the simple intervals form the major and minor intervals. These include seconds, thirds, sixths, and sevenths. A minor interval is one half-step smaller than a major one. They are described as follows:

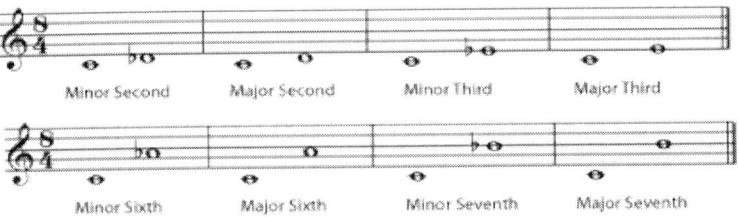

Figure 6.6

- Minor second – 1 half step
- Major second – 2 half steps
- Minor third – 3 half steps
- Major third – 4 half steps
- Minor sixth – 8 half steps
- Major sixth – 9 half steps
- Minor seventh – 10 half steps

- Major seventh – 11 half steps

Exercise 5

1. Give the complete name of the intervals.

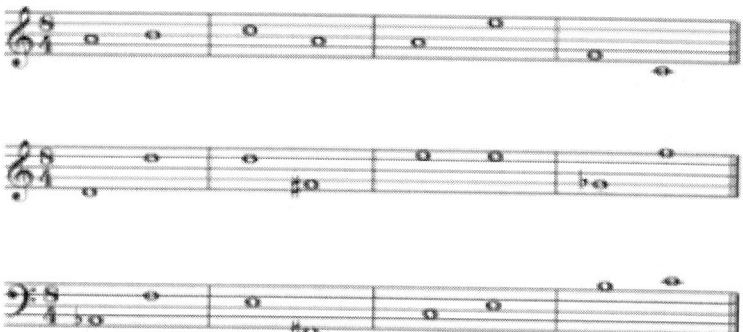

Chapter Summary

Here are the key points that you need to remember:

- Interval is the distance between two pitches.
- In order to name an interval, count the lines and spaces between the two notes. Don't forget to include the line or space the notes are standing on.
- The second phase of naming an interval must consider the half steps. The clef, key signature, and accidentals are important here.
- A simple interval is one octave or smaller, while a compound interval is greater than one octave.
- Intervals are considered perfect if their sound waves are closely related. Perfect intervals include primes, fourths, fifths, and octaves
- A perfect prime is also called unison.
- A minor interval is one half-step smaller than a major interval. These intervals include seconds, thirds, sixths, and sevenths.

In the next chapter, you will learn about key signatures and the circle of fifths.

Chapter Seven: Key Signatures

In this chapter, you will learn about how to use key signatures to make the performance of music much easier. You will also learn about the major and minor key signatures as well as how to read the circle of fifths.

Key signatures are a very important part of music. The key signature is what we use to know the pitches that a song will be performed. Every time that a piece of music is performed, it is played in a particular key or tonality. For example, if a song is to be played using the D key, then the entire song must be based around a D chord or a D note. Even the notes used will be from a D scale. The key signature represents all this information.

So how do we know the key that is being used?

If you look at the beginning of every line of written music, you will notice that there are sharps or flats (also known as accidentals) right after the clef symbol. These accidentals tell us the key to use. It is important to note that a key can either be a sharp or a flat, but it can never be both.

So, what is the significance of using keys? When you are writing a long piece of music in a single key, you will soon find it very tedious to keep repeating the accidentals all over the staff. Look at the image below to see what a simple melody in D major looks like if you don't use a key signature.

Figure 7.1

Now, this is just a short section of a piece of music. If you were writing a full song, the staff would get quite messy, not to mention the fact that you would get tired of writing all those sharps. So, to avoid this, music composers use key signatures only at the beginning of the staff to show the performers which pitches must have accidentals.

Below is the same simple melody in D major. But this time it has a key signature that indicates that the notes C and F should be sharpened.

Figure 7.2

The Circle of Fifths

This is a graphical way of arranging keys to show how closely related they are to each other. The circle of fifths has been part of music theory for centuries, and it provides a great method for summarizing the key signatures to be used for any key that has a maximum of seven sharps or flats.

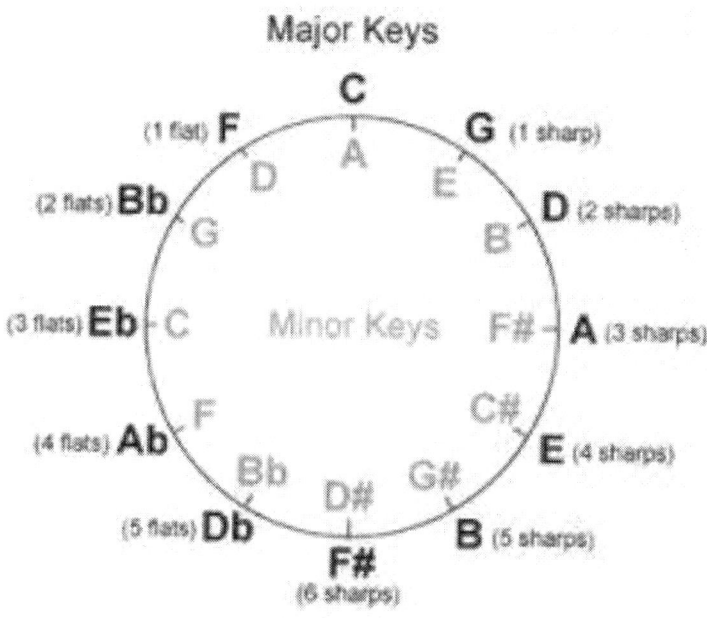

Figure 7.3

So how will you know which notes in the key are supposed to be sharpened or flattened? In order to use the circle of fifths to identify your key signature, you must use a mnemonic device to help you memorize the order of sharps and flats.

The first thing to do is memorize the order of notes on the following circle:

F C G D A E B

Most people use the mnemonic *Father Charles Goes Down And Ends Battle*

If you want to determine the sharp keys, you move clockwise around the circle of fifths. Then you read the mnemonic forward. For example, according to the circle of fifths, there are three sharps in the key A major. But which notes exactly are supposed to be sharp?

Moving clockwise along the circle and following the order of notes, you will identify the notes to be sharpened as F, C, and G.

If you want to determine the flat keys, you must move anticlockwise along the circle, and then read the mnemonic backward. For example, according to the circle of fifths, there are four flats in the key for A-flat major. But which notes should be flattened?

Moving anticlockwise along the circle and backward along the order of notes, you will see that B, E, A, and D are the notes that will have flats.

The reason why we call it a circle of fifths is because as you move from one section (or key) to the next, you are moving down or up by an interval of a perfect fifth. If you move clockwise by a perfect fifth, you will land on a key with one sharp more or one flat less than where you started. If you move anticlockwise a perfect fifth, you land on a key that has one flat more or one sharp less than where you started.

Minor Key Signatures

So far, we have been focusing more on the major keys. However, minor keys also have signatures. Every major key you see on the circle of fifths has a corresponding minor key with the exact same signature. Minor and major keys that have corresponding key signatures are referred to as ***relative keys***. For example, both F major and D minor have one flat. F major is regarded as the relative major of D minor while D minor is regarded as the relative minor of F major.

In other words, just because keys are next to each other on a keyboard (the chromatic scale) does not mean that they are closely related. The main factor that determines the relationship is having similar key signatures. The closer the keys are in the circle of fifths, the closer their relationship in terms of key signature.

This means that the next most closely related keys to F major and D minor are C major (or A minor), and B major (or G minor). Those keys that don't correspond at all with the key signature of F major are on the opposite side of the circle.

Exercise 6

1. Which keys in the circle of fifths are closely related to F sharp major and B flat major?

2. Name the major and minor keys for each key signature.

Chapter Summary

Here are the key points to remember:

- Key signatures tell us the pitches that a song will be performed in.
- To make writing music much easier, the key signature is placed at the beginning of the staff instead of between the notes in the staff.
- The accidentals indicate the key to be used in a piece of music.
- The circle of fifths is a graphical illustration of keys and indicates how closely related they are to each other.
- To determine the key being used, look at the number of sharps or flats in the key signature.
- To identify key signatures, use the mnemonic Father Charles Goes Down And Ends Battle (FCGDAEB).
- To identify the sharp keys, move clockwise around the circle and read the mnemonic forwards.
- To identify the flat keys, move anticlockwise and read the mnemonic backward.
- Major and minor keys that have corresponding key signatures are known as relative keys.

In the next chapter, you will learn about triads, chords, and chord progressions.

Chapter Eight: Building Chords

In this chapter, you will learn chords, which are the building blocks of the tone of a piece of music. Learning how to build chords can be a bit challenging for beginners, but the trick lies in taking it one step at a time. For that reason, we are going to focus on building triads, major chords, and minor chords.

Chords

A chord is simply a group of notes that are played together. Most of the sad songs you hear use what are known as minor chords. The upbeat songs tend to use suspended second chords or major seventh chords. Chords can either be used to make melodies or they can be arranged in specific sequences known as progressions to create a sense of direction and movement in music.

Triads

Chords are a set of three or more pitches that are played together. A chord that is made up of three notes that can be arranged as thirds is known as a ***triad***. The fastest way to know if a chord of three notes is a triad is to arrange the notes in a circle of thirds. If the pitch classes of the three notes sit next to each other, then they form a triad.

There are two ways of identifying a triad, i.e., according to its root and its quality. The ***root of chord,*** which is the note that gives the chord its name, is the lowest note. The second note in the triad is known as the ***third of chord***, while the last note in the triad is called the ***fifth of chord***. After you position the root of chord, you then place the third of chord a third higher than the root. The fifth of chord is then placed a fifth higher than the root, which coincides with a third higher than the third of chord. If you find this confusing, you may need to go to Chapter 6 (figure 6.3) where we learned about intervals.

In the figure below, the chord is written in the root position as a stack of third, which is the easiest way to write down a triad. Don't forget that in most cases, the root is the bottom note, unless you are dealing with an inversion.

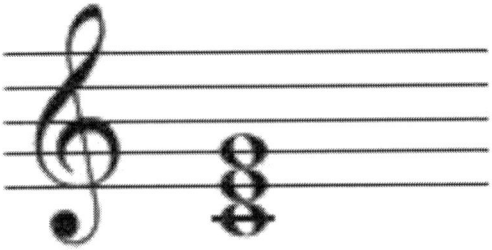

Figure 8.1

First and Second Inversions

First inversion occurs when the third of chord becomes the lowest note. In case the fifth of chord is placed at the bottom, then the chord is said to be in ***second inversion***. The second inversion is also known as a ***six-four chord*** because the intervals are a sixth and a fourth.

The most important factor in a chord is not the distance between the top two notes from the lowest note. The number of notes also isn't an issue. The thing that matters the most is which note is at the bottom.

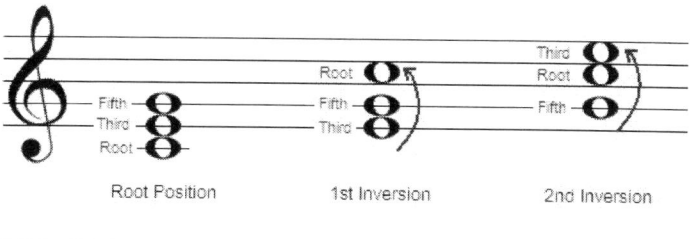

C Major Triad

Figure 8.2

Triad Qualities

The first step in determining the quality of a triad is to identify the interval between the root and the other notes in the chord. The four qualities of triads that can be found in major and minor scales include:

- Major triad – M3 and P5 above root
- Minor triad – m3 and p5 above root
- Diminished triad – m3 and d5 above root
- Augmented triad – M3 and A5 above root

The two most common triads are the major and minor chords. In these two types of chords, the root of the chord and fifth of chord are at an interval of a perfect fifth, which are 7 half steps. This interval can be split into a major third, which is 4 half-steps, and a minor third, which forms 3 half-steps.

A ***major chord*** is formed when the major third falls between the root and the third of chord. A ***minor chord*** is formed when the minor third falls between the root and the third of chord.

On the other hand, diminished and augmented chords do not have a perfect fifth, which explains why they produce an anxious feeling in listeners. **Augmented chords** are formed when two major thirds are combined, thus creating an augmented fifth. **Diminished chords** are formed when two minor thirds are combined, thus creating a diminished fifth.

Figure 8.3

Seventh Chords

This is a chord that is formed when you take a triad and combine it with a note that is a seventh above the root. There are many different varieties of seventh chords, and we distinguish them according to the type of seventh and type of triad used. Here are some of the most common types of seventh chords:

- Dominant seventh chord – This is a combination of a major triad and a minor seventh

- Minor seventh chord – This is a combination of a minor triad and a minor seventh

- Major seventh chord – This is a combination of a major triad and a major seventh

- Diminished seventh chord – This is a combination of a diminished triad and a diminished seventh

- Half-diminished seventh chord – This is a combination of a diminished triad and a minor seventh

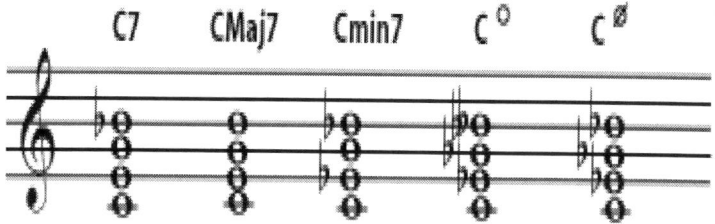

Figure 8.4

Exercise 7

1. Write these seventh chords – G minor seventh; B flat major seventh; F sharp minor seventh; and D diminished seventh.

Chapter Summary

Here are some of the key points that you need to remember:

- A chord is a group of notes that are played together.
- A chord that comprises three notes arranged as thirds is known as a triad.
- Its root and quality can identify a triad.
- In a triad, the lowest note is the root of chord; the second note is the third of chord, and the last note is the fifth of chord.
- First inversion occurs when the third of chord becomes the lowest note.
- Second inversion occurs when the fifth of chord becomes the lowest note.
- When the interval between the root and third of chord is the major third, a major chord is formed.
- When the interval between the root and third of chord is the minor third, a major chord is formed.

- When two major thirds are combined, an augmented chord is formed.
- When two minor thirds are combined, a diminished chord is formed.
- A seventh chord is formed when you add a triad and a note that is a seventh above the root.

Final Words

You have come to the end of the book. Though it was a long journey, I'm sure you now have a much better understanding of music theory than before. If you had never studied the subject previously, you should be ready to move on to the more complex theories of music. If you already had a background in music, then your knowledge of music theory will help you become an even better musician. For those who were seeking a refresher course in some of the elements you had forgotten, consider your mind refreshed.

Music theory is not really as hard as it looks or sounds. The bottom line is that you have to have a solid foundation that will always be there to guide you. The seven elements of music we have covered in this book are the keys to unlocking any musical composition. On top of that, there are seven good exercises in this book that will help you crystallize the knowledge you have gained in each chapter.

The questions provided in every exercise have covered the fundamentals that every music student and musician must know like the back of their hand. If you were keen when reading the book, I'm sure you had an easy time answering them. If you felt like you were struggling a little bit, then don't worry about it. Just go back to the chapter where you feel uncertain and reread it. Some of the concepts usually take time to sink in. Don't forget that the answers to every question are on the last page of the book.

Being able to read and write music is a very rewarding experience, and now you are ready to move onto the next phase of your musical journey. Yes, that was the easy part. Anybody can buy a book, read it, and toss it aside. All it will cost you is some time and money. However, you must now do the hard work necessary to integrate and incorporate this new knowledge into your music. This book has provided you with an opportunity to learn something that can help you going forward. Don't stop here. What is important is that you continue to practice and challenge yourself. Never stop learning and always make an effort to put into practice everything that you have learned in this book.

I am honoured that you took the time to read this book. It was a pleasure for me to walk with you through your musical journey. I hope you enjoyed reading and learning from this beginner's guide to music theory.

Thank you and good luck!

Solutions to Exercise Questions

Solutions to Exercise 1

1. Draw the staff on a piece of paper and practice writing the two clef symbols on the staff. Draw as many as you can until you learn it perfectly.

2. Draw the staff with a treble clef and name all the spaces on the staff.

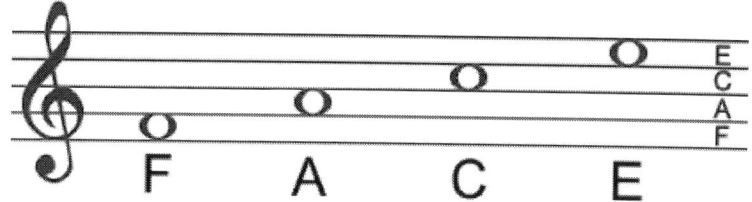

3. Draw the staff with a bass clef and name all the lines on it.

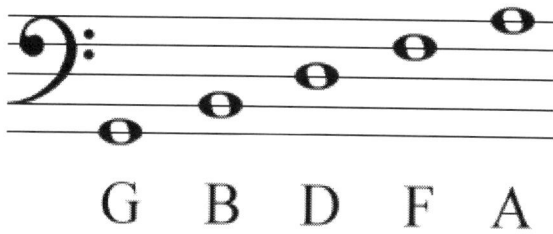

4. On a staff with a treble clef, name the ledger lines and spaces above the staff.

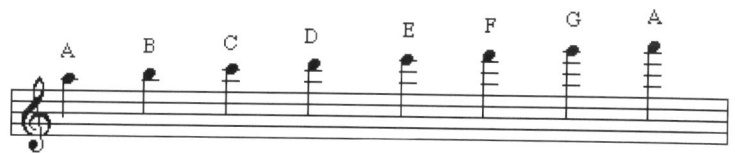

5. On a staff with a bass clef, name the ledger lines and spaces below the staff.

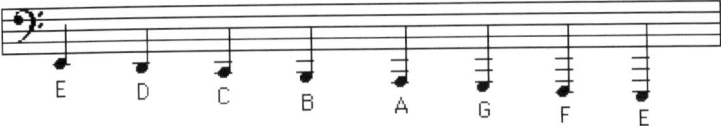

Solutions to Exercise 2

1. Complete the following series of natural notes: A B C D E F G A

2. Provide an alternative name for the following:

A♯ - B♭

D♭ - C♯

G♭ - F♯

E♭ - D♯

3. 1 semibreve = 8 quavers

4. 1 minim = 4 quarters

5. 1 minim = 1 quarter + 2 eighths

6. Three staves with a treble clef symbol and time signatures showing *two four time, three eight time,* and *six four time*. Fill in each measure with a different combination of note lengths. Use at least one dotted note per staff.

Solutions to Exercise 3

1. Italian tempo markings:

    - Poco piu mosso – a little more movement/motion

    - Piu vivo – more lively

    - Un poco allegro – a little fast

    - Molto adagio – very slow

2. In order from quietest to loudest: pp, mp, p, f, mf, ff

Solutions to Exercise 4

1. The staff with a treble clef and notes of the A major scale.

2. The staff with a bass clef and notes of the G flat major scale.

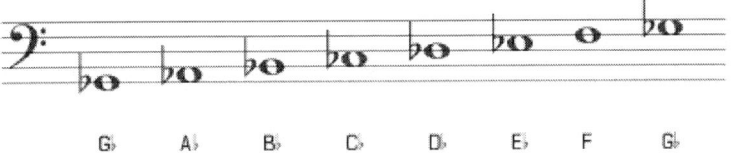

3. The staff with a treble clef and notes of the F minor scale.

F minor scale

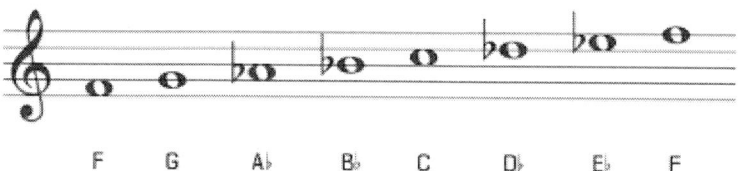

4. The staff with a treble clef and notes of the A flat minor scale.

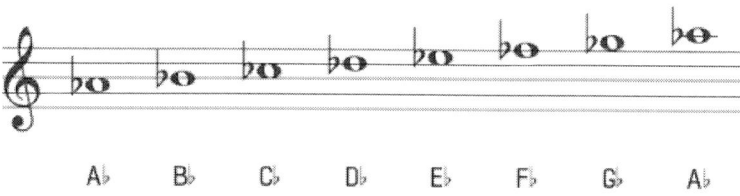

Solutions to Exercise 5

Names of intervals:

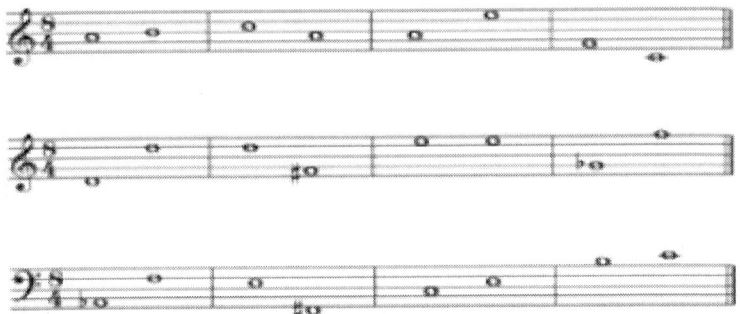

Top Staff:

Major Second - Minor Third - Perfect Fifth - Perfect Fourth

Centre Staff:

Perfect Octave – Minor Sixth – Perfect Prime (Unison) – Major Seventh

Bottom Staff:

Major Sixth – Minor Seventh – Major Third – Minor Second

Solution to Exercise 6

1. Relative keys to:

F sharp major – D sharp minor

B flat major – G minor

2. Major and minor keys for each key signature:

G Major – D Major – A Major – E Major

Solutions to Exercise 7

G minor 7th chord

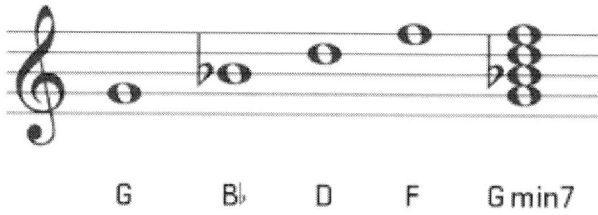

G   B♭   D   F   G min7

B-flat major 7th chord

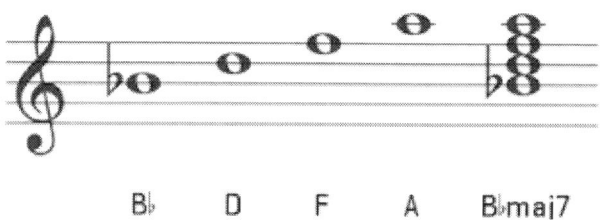

B♭   D   F   A   B♭maj7

F-sharp minor 7th chord

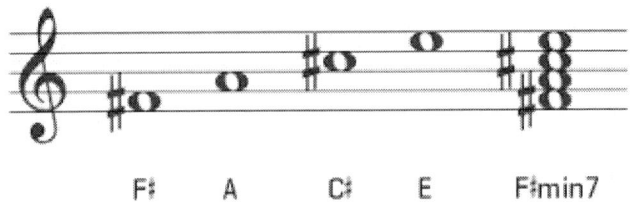

D diminished 7th chord

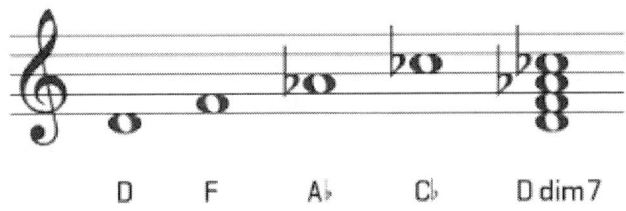

BOOK 2

HOW TO PLAY PIANO: IN 1 DAY

The Only 7 Exercises You Need to Learn Piano Theory, Piano Technique and Piano Sheet Music Today

Preston Hoffman

Table of Contents

Introduction 95
Chapter One: The Keyboard and Keys 97
Chapter Two: The Pedals 103
Chapter Three: Reading Sheet Music 107
Chapter Four: Practising Scales 121
Chapter Five: Adding in Chords 128
Chapter Six: Sharps and Flats 140
Chapter Seven: It's All About the Timing 145
Final Words 162

© Copyright 2017 - All rights reserved.

It is not legal to reproduce, duplicate, or transmit any part of this document by either electronic means or in printed format. Recording of this publication is strictly prohibited.

Introduction

Have you always wanted to learn to play the piano? Have you been hesitant about doing so because of the thought of having to spend endless hours practicing? Maybe you took some lessons but gave up because it was too hard.

What if there was a much easier way? What if I were to tell you that you could learn all the basics in seven simple lessons and that you could learn to play a proper tune in less than a day?

Does that sound a little too good to be true? Here are a couple more facts for you – playing the piano is not that complicated. It's just that the way that we are traditionally taught to play is a lot more complicated than it needs to be. Normally, you have to start by learning one note at a time, and have to learn all the theory before you get to actually start practicing what you have learned.

There is a lot of work to do before you even get close to seeing real results and that can be very disheartening.

What we do in this book is to break it down for you into simple but essential steps. You will learn the basics of music theory quickly and easily and will be able to play your first tune within hours. This will give you the motivation to carry on and keep practicing.

Will this book turn you into a maestro? No, but then it is not designed to do that. It will, however, get you started and teach you the foundations that you can build on.

You'll get to show your friends and family just how smart you are by being able to play your favorite songs – and save yourself a bundle in sheet music too.

If you are looking for an excellent introduction to playing the piano, this is the book for you. If you decide to carry on learning from there, this gives you a solid base to do that as well.

Chapter One: The Keyboard and Keys

In this chapter, you will learn about all the keys on the keyboard. This is the first step in our seven-point plan to teach you how to play the piano.

Your piano keyboard will look like this:

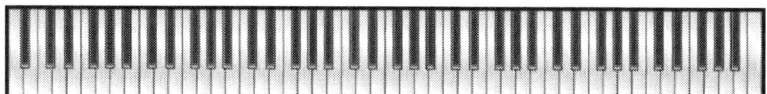

Looking down at the keyboard for the first time can be a bit intimidating. The keyboard is made up of a set of 52 white long keys, and a set of 36 shorter, more raised black keys. You should have 88 keys in total. (Some older pianos have smaller keyboards.)

Have a look at the diagram below – it is a smaller section of the keyboard, and contains all the basic information that you need to know. Once you get to know this information, you can basically apply it to the rest of the keyboard.

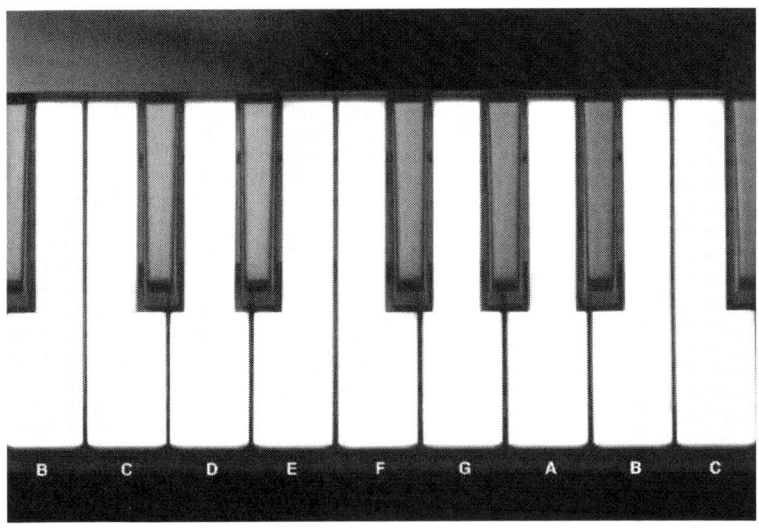

The White Keys

The white keys, as shown above, each play a particular note in music. These are named for the first seven letters of the alphabet – A through to G. There are a lot more keys than there are notes, so the letters are repeated over and over again. So, starting at the very left edge of the keyboard, you start with the letter A. The repetition makes it a lot easier – there are the same seven notes over and over again.

The next key represents the "B" chord, and so on, until you get to the key after the "G" chord. Then the keys start at "A" again. Each set represents one octave.

So, do you have to sit down and count each key from the start to determine which letter it represents? Fortunately, there is an easier way, and that is part of the reason that we have the black keys.

The black keys are divided into groupings of twos (twins) – marked in green on the diagram above or threes (triplets) – marked in red on the diagram above. The "C" note is always to the left of a set of twins. The "F" note is always to the left of a set of the triplets. To remember this more easily, you can think of the "C" as having two points to it and the "F" as having three points to it. From there, it is easy enough to fill in the remaining letters.

Whereabouts the keys are positioned on the board indicates how high or low the note is. The lowest notes are on the left, and you move up the scales as you move over to the right.

Quick Exercise: Play each key now and see how different they all sound. Find each of the "C" keys on the keyboard. Follow with all of the "D" keys and so on. Then play the following notes on any set of the keys:

B, D, B, E, D, B.

Do you recognize the tune at all? Does it remind you of when you were a kid? It should – it's the start of "It's Raining, It's Pouring." Well done, you have just played a tune without a single music sheet in sight. Didn't I tell you that this was going to be easy?

Play it again in a different octave so that you can hear how it sounds higher or lower. Repeat on all the different octaves to note the differences in sound.

The Black Keys

The black keys are different musical notes to the white keys. Play them, and you will notice a distinct difference. The names of these keys are also the same letters of the alphabet and take on the names of the white keys nearest them. The distinction is that keys to the left of the white key are known as flats and to the right of the white key are known as sharps. So, you have "B Sharp" or "B Flat," for example.

An easy way to remember this is to think about how your cutlery is laid out on the table. Your knife is sharp and always laid out to the right of your plate. That makes it easy to remember that right is sharp.

Now, because the black keys have a white key on either side of them, they can be called sharps or flats interchangeably. If you look to the right of a white "B" key on your keyboard, the black key is "C Sharp." But it is also left of the white "D" key and so is "D Flat." Don't overthink it too much – it is not all that important right now, and we go into it in more detail in Chapter 6 anyway.

What is more important is to learn your way around the keyboard – think more in terms of the letter, rather than it being a sharp or flat.

Quick Exercise: Now you know how to find your "C" and "F" notes and, because of this, how to find the others as well. Play each "C" note on the black and white keys and listen to how each sounds. Do the same for all the other keys as well.

Now try something a little more complicated. Position your thumb over any white key and your forefinger over the corresponding black key. Play each in quick succession. Then try playing them together. Experiment a little until you find the tones that match one another more closely.

Intervals

These are the distance between the different notes. A semitone, or half-step, will always separate the black key from the white key next to is. Where the white keys are not broken by black keys, like between "B" and "C" or "E" and "F", the difference in the note is a semitone.

A full tone is the space between two white keys that have a black key in between them, like "C" and "D".

Chapter Summary

- Your keyboard is made up of 52 white keys and 36 black keys. (Some older keyboards have fewer keys.)
- Each key represents a particular musical note.
- There are seven musical notes that we use in music – these are named A through to G.

- The black keys are grouped in twins or triplets to help you locate the different notes more easily.
- The white key to the left of a twin is always "C." The white key to the left of a triplet is always an "F."
- To remember the difference, remember that "C" has two points to it and "F" has three to it.
- The black keys take their names from the white keys closest to them.
- The black key to the right of a white key is called sharp. The one to the left of a white key is called flat.
- An easy way to remember this is that knives are sharp and are always put to the right of your plate when the table is laid.
- Intervals refer to the difference in sound between the white and black keys.

In the next chapter, you will learn about the pedals on your piano and how to use them.

Chapter Two: The Pedals

In this chapter, you will learn how and when to use the pedals on your piano. This is the second step in our seven-point plan in helping you learn to play the piano.

The pedals on the piano are not just there for decoration. You use the pedals for sounds that are not possible using just your hands. Most standard pianos will have two such foot pedals – the Una Corda on the left and the Sustain on the right. Some pianos have three pedals. The extra pedal in the middle is called the Sostenuto, but it is seldom used.

The Una Corda Pedal (The Soft Pedal)

Use your left foot to play this pedal. It helps to soften notes, so could be used when you are first starting to build up to a crescendo. It will not work on very loud notes, so the range is limited somewhat.

The Sustain Pedal

You will use your right foot with this pedal. It elongates your note's sound and causes it to resonate after you have lifted your fingers from the key. The resonance will be held until you take your foot off the pedal. This is usually used to bridge harmonies. With this pedal, as long as you are pressing the pedal, all the notes you play will be sustained.

The Sostenuto

As mentioned before, this is not something that you will use very often. You would normally use your right foot to play it, and it is similar to the Sustain Pedal in that it sustains the notes played. The difference between this pedal and the previous one is that the Sostenuto pedal only sustains the notes that you were playing when you pressed the pedals. Any notes played after that will play as normal.

Using the Pedals

When you start playing, get into position and position the balls of your feet above the pedals. Your heels should still touch the ground; this will help you maintain a good posture and also allow you to keep a light touch when it comes to depressing the pedals.

What you need to keep in mind is that this is not a stomping contest. You need to practice lifting your foot off the pedals gently. If you take your foot off too quickly, it can create a noisy bang; It can take a little practice to get used to using the pedals smoothly. Just think of it like parking your car – you don't smash the accelerator to the ground when parking, you ease into the parking slowly.

If the music calls for the use of the pedal, you will see the word "Ped" marked where you need to apply the pedal. Alternatively, the composition may call for the use of it all the way through the piece. You can release the pedal when you see an asterisk on the sheet. This will look like:

Quick exercise: Try using the pedals in conjunction with the lines of "It's Raining it's Pouring" that you learned in the previous chapter. Mix it up a little, play the same tune using the Una Corda pedal from time to time and then listen to how it sounds when you use the Sustain pedal instead. If you do have a Sostenuto panel, play around with that one as well.

Chapter Summary

- Most pianos have two pedals – the Una Corda pedal and the Sustain pedal.
- Some pianos have a third pedal – the Sostenuto pedal.
- The Una Corda pedal is always on the left; the Sustain pedal is always on the right. If the Sostenuto pedal is there, it will be in the middle.
- You will not use the Sostenuto pedal very often.
- The Una Corda pedal helps to soften notes.
- The Sustain pedal keeps the notes going for as long as you have the pedal down. It will do this for all notes played, while the pedal is down.
- The Sostenuto pedal isolates the note that was played when the pedal was first pressed and sustains only that particular note. The rest are played as normal.

In the next chapter, you will learn how to read some basic sheet music for yourself.

Chapter Three: Reading Sheet Music

In this chapter, you will learn what many of those dots and lines mean when it comes to sheet music. This is the third quick step in the program.

You need to know something about reading music in order to progress. Think of sheet music like a script for a movie, except that it is written using musical symbols rather than words. The composer could, technically, write out the words but it would make playing the music much slower and difficult because you would have to read each word.

Symbols are a lot easier to read, once you understand what they mean. The composer tells you which notes you should play, when to pause, how long to pause for, and even the pace at which you should play.

A sheet of music will look something like this:

Everything You Need to Know About a Piano Score

If you look at the score above, you will see a lot of dots, dashes, and other symbols. It looks a little confusing, but it's not so bad if you take it a note at a time. Each of the notes tells you which key you need to play and how long you need to play it for.

To keep the notes in some semblance of order, they are written on a five-line stave.

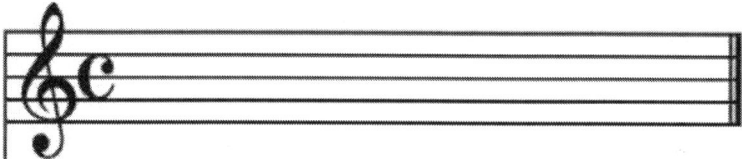

Starting with the Stave

The notes can be placed on the lines, or in the spaces between lines. Each line or space represents a specific note. The notes are divided up into equal sections called measured. These are separated from one another by bar lines – vertical lines at the end of that particular measure. The stave will normally start with some type of clef (The stylized "G" in the illustration above), and this may be followed by a sharp or a flat (The "C" in the illustration above.)

In addition, the markings above the stave will usually tell you what speed to play at. The markings underneath the stave will tell you what volume that section is to be played at.

You will see that there are usually two staves joined together with brackets, with different symbols at the top and bottom. This is known as a grand stave. It is denoted like this because you need to play both staves together – one set being the notes to play with your right hand, the other the notes to play with your left hand.

Don't worry about this too much at this stage – the main tune is usually shown in the stave for the right hand, so you don't need to pay attention to both now. In fact, as you will see later, you don't even have to have these two to play a tune so if you find it confusing, don't stress about it. We have a way around that.

The Basic Symbols to Learn

The Treble Clef

This is the stylized G that we were talking about in the previous section. There are a number of different ways that this is written. The treble clef shown below will denote which keys you need to play with your left hand. X

The treble clef looks like:

The Base Clef

This shows the part of the music to be played with your left hand. (To start out with, we are not going to worry too much about the left-hand section.) The base clef looks like:

The Key Signature

This is another thing that might appear at the start of the music. It shows which of the notes need to be played as flats and which need to be played as sharps.

This is what this will look like on your sheet music:

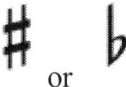

The Time Signature

This can be any two numbers. The numbers tell you how many beats there are in each measure. (We go over this in more detail in Chapter Seven.) This will look like:

$$\frac{2}{2}$$

Tempo Marking

This is a way of showing you what tempo the piece should be played at. The notation below shows the number of crotchet beats to play in a minute. Alternatively, they could write out what speed the piece is to be played at. This will often be in Italian like "Presto". (We go over each of these in more detail in Chapter 7).

This will look like:

♩=130

Dynamics

This lets you know what volume you need to play at. The "P" in the above diagram means Piano, or quiet. The "F" in the above means Forte or loudly. If the symbol has an "M" after it, it means moderate volume. (We are not really going to worry too much about that in these lessons though.) These symbols look like:

The Notes

These relate to the actual notes that you are playing so let's go into them in a little more detail. A note is generally made up of a head (the dot) and a stem, the vertical line that is either above or below the dot. Your notes will look something like:

Whole Notes

This is a whole note and will be one of the only ones that doesn't have a vertical line. This is meant to last four beats.

Half Notes

These are half notes or minimums and are played for two beats. You can tell that they are half notes because the dot is not filled in.

Quarter Notes

These are quarter notes – you will normally play four of these in one measure. (More about that in Chapter Seven).

Quavers and Semi-Quavers

These are eighth notes or quavers and sixteen notes or semiquavers.

Where the Notes Are Displayed

There are two shortcuts that you can use to remember which line or space each note is displayed in. Remember how we said that some of the notes are displayed on the lines, and some are displayed in the spaces in between them, this is how you remember what notes go where.

For The Lines

Remember the mnemonic device, Every Good Boy Deserves Fruit. In this case, the "E" note is recorded on the top line, the "G" note on the next line down, the "B" note on the middle line, the "D" note on the next line down and the "F" note on the final line.

For The Spaces

Remember the word FACE to keep this one straight but this time start from the space at the bottom and work your way up. So, the "F" note is in the final space of the stave, the "A" note is in the next space up, the "C" note is in the space second from the top, and the "E" note is in the space right at the top of the stave. In this case, the "F" note is an octave lower than in the previous example.

A Quick Shortcut

I am now going to teach you a shortcut to playing popular music. This only works with music that has words to it, but it is a great shortcut and is more than enough if you just want to be able to play some tunes for the family.

The sheet music example we displayed previously was made up of grand staves. When you have lyrics as well, these are displayed in the vocal line. This is a stave that is directly above the grand staves and is a much more simplified version of the notes. It will usually have a treble stave at the very front.

If you want to start playing music quickly and easily, concentrate on the vocal line only. This allows you to play at the pace that suits you and is a lot easier than having to read the more complex staves beneath it.

The additional advantage of doing this is that you can buy music sheets that only have the vocal line on them. If your main aim is to be able to play a few tunes, this can save you a lot of money and space because the grand staves are not usually included in these copies.

Quick Exercise: Go to http://www.music-for-music-teachers.com/silent-night-sheet-music.html, and you can download the sheet music for "Silent Night" for free, in a simple format. It's a fairly simple composition and one that you probably already know the melody for. See how well you can follow along on your piano.

Chapter Summary

- You need to know what the different symbols on sheet music are in order to be able to interpret it.
- Sheet music is set out in a five-line stave. You can see which note to play based on where it is placed in the stave and also the symbol used.
- Things like the general tempo of the piece will be listed at the beginning of the stave.
- Notations above and below the stave can show the speed at which a piece is to be played and what volume to play it at.
- A stave will usually consist of at least two separate sections, one for the notes to be played with the left hand and one for the notes to be played with the right hand. These two staves should be played at the same time and so are bracketed together to form a grand stave. (We are not going to do that right now, though.)
- The symbol for the note will tell you what note to play and how long to play it for.
- Each note is displayed on a different line, or space, in the stave.
- An easy way to remember which note goes on which line is to remember "Every Boy Deserves Good Fruit." This is read from the top line to the bottom one.
- An easy way to remember which note goes into what space, is to remember the word "FACE." In this case, the spaces are read from the bottom up. The notes used in this case are an octave lower than in the previous instance.

- To make things a lot easier for yourself, you can read the music from the vocal line. This is a much more simplified stave meant to be read by singers so it does not have all the symbols a grand stave would have and does not have them separated into notes to be played by the left hand and notes to be played by the right hand.

In the next chapter, you will learn about more about practicing scales and why it is not a boring time waster.

Chapter Four: Practising Scales

In this chapter, you will learn about scales and why you should look forward to practicing them. This is your fourth lesson – you are almost there now.

Now that you understand about which keys are which, know when to use the pedals and know something about reading sheet music, we are ready to move on to playing scales. This is the fourth step in our program.

How did you do with playing "Silent Night?" It should have been relatively simple for you – you might have made a mistake or two here or there, but, overall, you should have been able to follow it. See how easy it is to start playing real music? And you can play popular songs like that without ever having to worry about learning scales.

However, there is a good reason that one of the first things you normally learn to play on a piano are scales. Now, admittedly, this can seem a little boring, but it is good practice. Scales are a great way for you to build up a working knowledge of the melodies in a song and to also give your fingers more practice. So, while you can play without practicing scales, if you really want to start getting better, you will have to spend some time on this.

The most important thing about scales is that you should repeat them over and over again. Think of it like a putting green in golf – you are there to practice your swing, not to actually play a game. The more you practice, however, the better your swing gets and the better you are able to play when you actually head out to the course. The same applies for practicing scales on your piano.

What is a Scale?

It is a series of notes that follow on from one another in a particular order. The most commonly encountered scales are major scales and minor scales. They both have the following commonalities:

- They are both eight notes in length.
- The topmost note and the bottommost note are only an octave apart.
- Each note is done in order from lowest to highest or highest to lowest. You do not mix up the order of the notes at all.
- Scales are made up of a combination of half- or whole steps.

If you understand how the scales work, you are able to build any type of scale you want, just by adding in the right sequence of steps. Scales form the basis for creating chords and allowing you to learn to improvise. You will need to know these if you want to start composing your own music.

The scales that you choose to practice will be dependent on what musical style you are most interested in. It is, however, a good idea to start by learning the major scales and then move on to practicing the minor scales.

Major Scales

The pattern here will be a tone, a tone, a semitone, a tone, atone, a tone, and a semitone. It is pretty easy to work out, as long as you start on the right note. All major scales will be based on the same principle.

You can, for example, play an "C" scale in major. You can start on "C" and then move up through the other notes, using only the white keys. The "C" major scale is one of the easiest to start with because you only need to concentrate on the white keys.

Major scales are generally thought to be livelier in nature.

Minor Scales

Once you are more comfortable with major scales, you can try your hand at minor scales. The minor scales are available in three separate versions – the harmonic or the natural or the melodic scales. What this means is that every minor scale has three separate formats to learn.

The Natural Minor Scales

This is the key minor scale to practice. The difference between it and your major scale is that you start with the A note and then finish off again with the A note.

The Harmonic Minor Scales

This also follows a set pattern, but it is slightly different. It is a tone, a semitone, a tone, a tone, a semitone, a tone + a half and a semitone. This pattern is often described as a bit eerie in nature and will lend something of a haunting quality to your work.

The Melodic Minor Scales

This is more complex because you will use the pattern, a tone, a tone, a semitone, atone, a tone, a semitone and then a tone when working your way up the scales. When working your way back, it changes to a tone, a tone, a semitone, a tone, a tone, a semitone, and finishes on tone.

What makes this scale useful, is that it teaches you to be more flexible when it comes to your other scales. When practicing your minor scales, it is best to start with the A minor scales because these are easiest.

Quick Exercise: Practice this now - find the Middle C and practice working your way through all seven notes. You would start by using your thumb and the rest of the fingers on your right hand and then bring in your left hand for the final two keys. Practice this working your way up the scales, and then down them again.

When you have mastered that, you can move on to practicing more scales. You can try starting with a different note, always remembering to move up either half a step or a whole step. Here is an illustration of the different C Scales that you can use to get you started with your practicing.

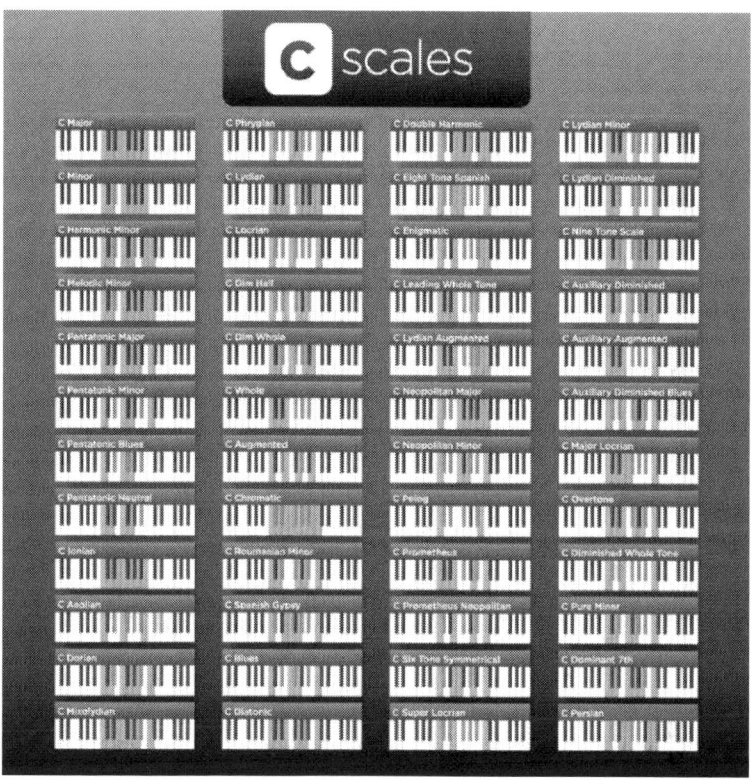

Most of the C scales shown above can be accomplished using your right hand only. It is also important to practice scales using your left hand, so don't just focus on one type. Try to practice at least three different scales a day for at least ten minutes overall in order to get better at them.

Chapter Summary

- Scales are seen by a lot of people as boring, but they are essential exercises when it comes to getting to know the keys.
- They can also be used as warmups or to help build up the strength in your finger.
- The key to getting scales right is to know your intervals really well. Every successive key is either a half- or whole step up or down from the previous one.
- There are minor scales and major scales, each with their own unique pattern.
- There are three varieties of minor scales – the natural, harmonic and melodic.

In the next chapter, you will learn about using chords to make the melodies sound richer.

Chapter Five: Adding in Chords

In this chapter, you will learn about adding in chords. This is the fifth step in the program.

Chords are important in creating harmonies. You will distinguish them on your music sheet because they will have three or four notes stacked on top of one another.

What is a Chord?

A chord is made up of at least three tones, played simultaneously, where the intervals are based on a set formula. So, slamming your fingers down on four or five random keys may be fun, but is not a chord.

Three-Note Chords

These are the simplest ones to work with and are also known as triads. You will normally play these by using your pinky, thumb, and forefinger. Chords begin very simply. Like melodies, chords are based on scales.

Chords are essentially based on scales, the difference being that with scales, each note is played in succession. With chords, all of the notes are played together.

The root note is the note that you start with. The chord will be named for this note. If you are using a basic triad, you will have your root note and two other notes, notes that are at a third interval from the first note and at the fifth interval from the first note.

You can add to the chord by moving up a step or a half-step, or by adding extra notes in. To make things easier for you, though, I have included a list of all the basic chords at the end of this chapter.

Major Chords

These are the ones that you will use most often and are the easiest to play. A lot of the songs that you play, including Silent Night, consist of major chords. Major chords are based on your major scales. The first example in the illustration below is an example of a major chord.

Most of the time, composers will omit writing "Major" when using a chord. They simply use the symbol for chord above the staff of it to show which chord it is. If you see the symbol for a chord, and nothing naming it, you can assume that it is a major chord.

Other Chords You May Encounter

You are mostly going to be dealing with major or minor chords, but that does not mean that these are all that there is. Other chords are formed by adding extra notes to your standard major or minor chord.

Augmented Chords And Diminished Chords

The only real difference in a major or minor chord is the third interval. The fifth interval, however, is always the same and it is here that you can play around to create a new chord altogether.

Augmented chords consist of the root note, your major third interval, and an augmented fifth interval. With augmented chords, you raise the final note by another half-step and always work with a major chord to start with. Here are examples of augmented chords.

Piano Chords — Augmented

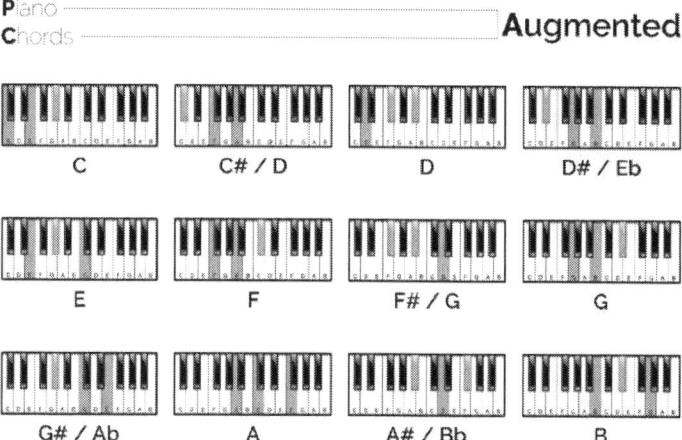

Diminished chords consist of the root note, your minor third interval, and your diminished fifth interval. In this case, you lower the final note by half a step and always work with a minor chord to start with. You would normally see them with "Dim" in the name.

Here are some examples of diminished chords:

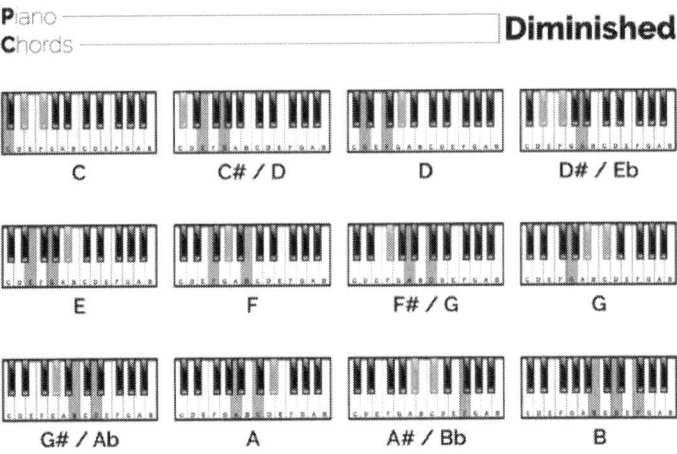

Suspended Chords

This is considered a three-note chord, but it is not really a triad. In this case, one of the notes is left hanging, meaning that you need to wait for the next one. There are two options when it comes to suspended chords – The second and fourth suspended chords. They will have "Sus" in the name.

A suspended two chord is made up of the root note, the major second interval, and the fifth interval. A suspended four chord is made up of the root note, the fourth interval, and the fifth interval.

Generally speaking, a suspended chord will usually be followed by another note, but they can also be used on their own.

Here are examples of suspended chords:

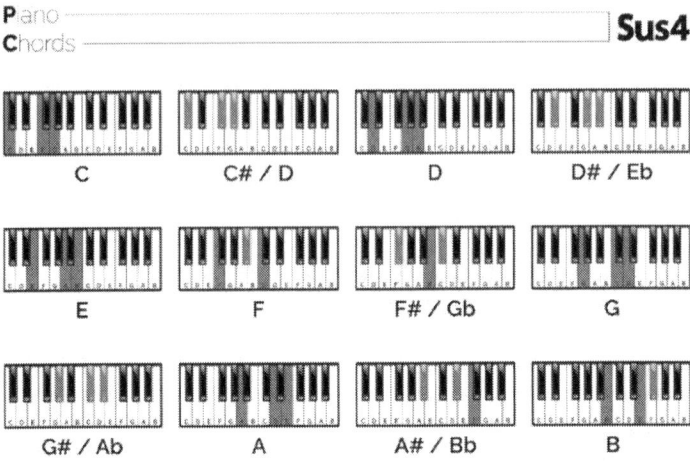

Adding a Seventh Interval

A triad is a basic kind of chord. In order to make it more interesting, you can add other notes at the end in the form of a seventh interval. It is usually used in a composition to help create suspense and will usually be followed by a major chord or minor chord. On its own, it is not likely to sound great, but when added to a triad, it improves the sound.

You can choose to add any of the chords we have discussed here to create this seventh interval.

The Chord Symbols

Chord symbols let you know the type of chord and what the root note of the chord is. These will start with the letter of the root note. (Keep in mind that with a major chord, this will be all there is.)

With other chords, you will have either a letter in the name, such as "M" to indicate a minor chord and/ or a letter like "7" to indicate the seventh chord. So, if, for example, you see the name Dm6, you know you have that you are playing the D minor chord with a sixth interval.

The chord is played along with the note that is shown underneath it. You will hold this chord until you see a new chord symbol or change of cord marked in the music.

Chord Inversions

It's not the most interesting exercise to play the same chords over and over again. You really don't need to do this at all. It doesn't matter what you do with the basic chords; they will always sound exactly the same.

That is where chord inversions come into play. They allow you to change up the sound of a chord. So instead of playing the root chord, and following it with the third chord and fifth chord, as usual, you could change things up by starting with the final chord and ending on the root chord. So now what you are doing is to play the root chord an octave higher than the standard chords.

Inversions can also help you to transition from one chord to the next. Let's say you are playing a C major chord, followed by an A minor chord. This would mean playing the C chord and then moving your hand over to play the next set of keys – it would be somewhat clumsy.

If you use an inversion, though, your hand will end up in the correct position as you end off the C chord, allowing you to play with a lot less effort.

Using Chord Progressions

Chord progression means moving through a range of chords in the same key signature. Imagine how boring it would be if you played the same chord throughout the entire piece. You can use chord progressions to liven things up a bit or to move from one signature to the next.

Arpeggios

You don't always have to play the notes that make up your chord at the same time. You can also rather play them one after another in sequence. Arpeggios help to keep the piece moving. You would, for example, instead of playing a typical C major chord, play each note, starting with the "C," individually. You would then play the "C" in the next octave before reversing the order of play and going back down to the first "C" you played.

This would just be one possible version so try changing it up a bit. This is also possible using minor chords – you just would not need to descend at the end of the structure again.

A Round-Up of Different Chords That You Might Come Across

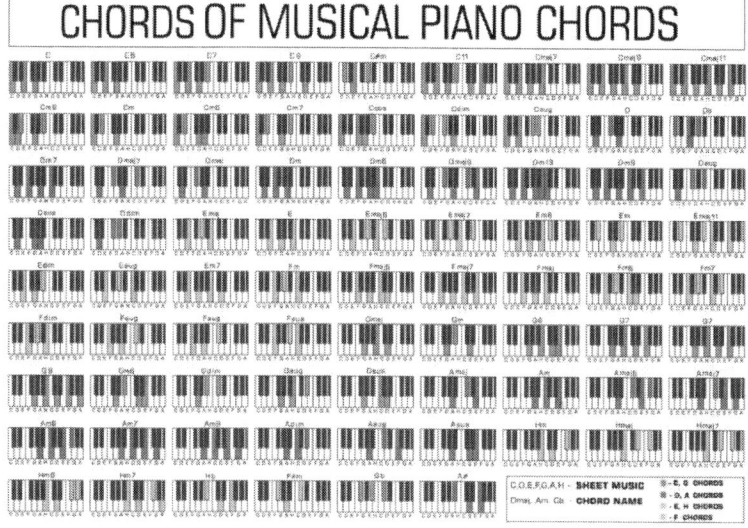

Chapter Summary

- Chords are notes that are played together to create a more harmonious composition.
- On the music sheet, a chord is denoted if there are three notes stacked together.
- Chords are at least three notes long and are calculated according to set formulae rather than just being chosen at random.
- A chord is usually based on the scales that you use.
- There are many different kinds of chords.
- Augmented chords are created from major scales and have the last note going up by half a step.
- Diminished chords are created from minor scales and have the last note dropping by half a step. They will have "Dim" in their name.
- Suspended chords leave you hanging and need to be finished off with another note. They will have "Sus" in their name.
- You can add another interval in order to make the chord more interesting.
- Major chords are named after their root note. So, a C major cord is simply named "C."
- You can invert cords to make them more interesting and to make the play smoother. This means starting with your top note and carrying on into the next octave with your root note.

- Chord progressions can make the piece more interesting and can help bridge one signature line with another.
- Arpeggios are another way to change things up – you play exactly the same notes, except this time you change things up by playing the notes in sequence rather than together.

In the next chapter, you will learn more about sharps and flats.

Chapter Six: Sharps and Flats

In this chapter, you will learn how to start incorporating the black keys and how to recognize when to do so. This is your sixth lesson.

The symbols that we deal with in this chapter are also known as accidentals. These "accidentals" tell you when to use the black keys, or how to modify your note's pitch.

As mentioned previously, the black keys are called sharps or flats, and named for the white keys directly next to them. Let's do a quick recap. If the black key is to the right of the white key, it will be that key's sharp. If it is to the left of that key, it will be that key's flat.

Here's a diagram of how this would look on your actual keyboard:

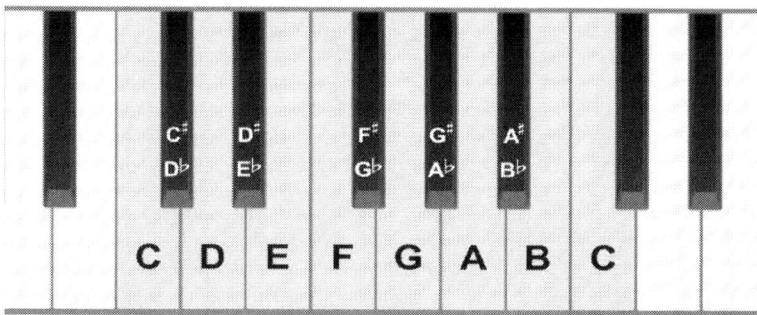

On the sheet music, you will see the symbol for the sharp or the flat directly before the note, next to the head of the note that it applies to.

Sharps

Sharps raise the pitch by a half-step or semitone. The symbol for a sharp is:

♯

Flats

Flats lower the pitch by a half-step or semitone. The symbol for a flat is:

♭

The Natural Key

This tells you that it is time to stop using the black keys. It will precede the natural note and tell you that you should play all the remaining notes in that series as natural notes. The symbol for the natural key is:

The Key Signature

You will also see these notes directly after the clef or base staves and before any time signature. This is what is referred to as the key signature, and it lets you know what key to use for the tune, and how many sharps and flats there are in the piece. You will need to look this over before starting.

Once you have been practicing your scales, this gets a whole lot simpler to do. All of the keys except for A minor and C major have both flats and sharps.

Chapter Summary

- Accidentals are used to change the pitch of notes – they change the pitch by a half-tone or semitone.
- The three accidentals are Flat, Sharp and Natural.
- To get the flat and sharp notes, you have to use the black keys on the keyboard.
- The flat takes its name from the white key to its left and reduces the pitch.
- The sharp takes its name from the black key to its right and increases the pitch.
- So, every black key is both a sharp and a flat.
- The natural symbol tells you to revert to stop using the black keys.

In the next chapter, you will learn why timing is so important and how you can get this critical aspect right.

Chapter Seven: It's All About the Timing

In this chapter, you will learn the final and possibly most important element in this book – how to get the timing right. This is the final step in our program.

There is more to music than getting the notes and chords right. (Sure, that is obviously a big piece of the puzzle, but you also need to be able to get the timing and beat right.) In fact, you might be able to slip an incorrect chord or note past your audience without them noticing, but they will notice immediately if your timing is off.

The timing of the notes is what makes the music happy or sad. If we never adjusted the tempo at which we played, every piece of music would sound pretty much the same. Each note has a point where it starts and a point where it ends. As a result, we need to assign values to this length that we are able to count. In this chapter, we are going to learn how to really get the rhythm going and keep it going.

The Beat

When you are listening to music and clapping along or tapping your foot in time with it, the beat is what you are trying to keep up with. The faster the beat, the faster and more energetic the song. The slower the beat, the slower the music is. Getting the tempo, or how fast the beat is, right is extremely important.

Use Tempo to Measure the Beat

When it comes to music, time gets measured in beats. In this case, the number of beats per minute. If you want a piece to sound correct, you need to pay attention to the beat.

Quick Exercise: Get out your smartphone and set the timer for a minute. Every two seconds, tap your foot once. That's a beat. Now, you can speed this up by increasing the number of taps to one per second, or slow it down to one tap every three seconds. That's the tempo.

In the exercise above, the first beat was 30 beats per minute because you tapped your foot 30 times. The second beat was 20 beats per minute because you slowed it down. In both cases, the beat was steady because you were timing your taps to the second.

When reading music, you would refer to the tempo marking to tell you what speed to play the music at. This will either be in the form of either a written word to tell you what pace to use, or a metronome marking that will tell you exactly how many beats per minute.

You can follow the guidelines in the table below to see what the basic readings are in terms of tempo.

Written	Translation	Number of Beats Per Minute
Largo	Very Slow	40 – 60
Adagio	Slow	61 - 72
Andante	Moderate	73 – 96
Allegro	Fast	97 - 132
Vivace	Faster	133 – 168
Presto	Very Fast	169 - 208

Measuring Tempo

When you are playing a piece of music, you won't be able to check your smartphone to see how many seconds have elapsed. A metronome is a handy device that can help you instead. You set it to the rate that you like, and it will tick out the rhythm accordingly.

The Grouping of Beats

Remember how I said earlier that the sheet of music was like a script? Every note is recorded in the order that it is meant to be played in. Unlike a script, however, the stave can be divided up into equal sections of time. These smaller sections make it possible to check the beat and to understand whereabouts you are in the actual composition.

Now, in a slower tempo song, this might not be much of a problem, but when it comes to faster-paced music, you could have a few hundred different beats in just a few minutes. Keeping track of the beat in this manner would mean counting high numbers when you are trying to concentrate on what you are doing.

It would become difficult to do this, so composers have come up with a workaround. Instead, the music is divided up into measures – smaller bits that are easier to keep track of. The number of beats in a measure will normally be decided by the composer, and this can change. They will indicate the end of a measure by drawing a vertical line, or bar line, through all the lines and spaces of the stave. This will look something like:

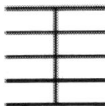

Most compositions, however, will have four beats per measure. This means that you would just have to count to four each time when playing – not too difficult a task. The measures break the music into segments or patterns that we can then use to help determine the time signature of the piece.

The Rhythm of Melody

Without the melody of notes played, the beat wouldn't mean much at all. The different lengths of the notes are what makes the music more interesting. It's like listening to a good public speaker – they change the cadence of their voice and mix up the tones so that it sounds more interesting.

In contrast, if the speaker just spoke in a monotone, without varying the tone or rhythm, it wouldn't be long before everyone became bored with the speech. The same is true of music.

Some music is very distinctive – you can recognize the tune just by hearing the beat. Take "Jingle Bells" for example – you don't have to hear it being played on an instrument to recognize it, you could tap out the beat with your foot, and someone would still recognize it.

We said earlier that you could get away with not having to read all the characters on a standard music sheet. You do, however, need to know exactly how much time every note is meant to last for. At the beginning of the piece, the composer lets you know how many equal pieces to divide each measure into. That means working out fractions but, in this case, it's not hard.

Think of it like cutting up a pizza. You can divide the pizza up into halves, quarters or eighths, or more if you like. When it comes to music, this usually translates into four pieces of "pizza" per measure. Or, more accurately, four quarter notes, or four beats. This is represented by the most common music symbol:

♩♩

You will always know if a note is a quarter note because the head will always be completely black. In our example, you have divided the pizza up into four equal slices and are eating just one, so it is finished faster. In the same way, the notes are played faster and not held for as long.

Quick Exercise: Set your metronome to one beat per second. Every time it clicks, play one-quarter note in whichever key you prefer. Stick to a single note, for now, say for example, "C" so that you can get the hang of playing to the beat. Every time the metronome clicks, hit the "C" key. Get this right before moving on to the next section.

Half Notes

Alternatively, you could choose to divide the pizza into halves and eat one piece again. You will take longer to eat the pizza because there is more of it. By a similar token, half notes are longer than quarter notes, so you would divide the measure up into two instead of four. So, it would now be two beats per measure instead of just one.

This would be represented on the sheet as follows:

♩ ♩

Quick Exercise: Set your metronome to one beat per second again, and this time, play a note on every second click. You would hold the key down for the count of these two beats.

Why do the Stems Get Displayed Differently?

You will notice in the examples above, that there are two ways to show the stem of a note – either pointing up or pointing down. Why is that? Any notes that are either on the middle line of the stave or above it, will have their stems underneath the note head and to the right. Any notes that fall below this will have the stems above the note head and to the left.

This helps to make a clearer distinction between the notes on different lines. If all the notes were just circles, it would be a lot harder to keep your place when reading the music quickly.

Whole Notes

A whole note lasts the entire measure for a count of four. So, back to our pizza example, if you ate the whole thing, it would take longer.

It is a simple circle and looks like this:

o

Playing a whole note is pretty simple, just count to four and then play the note. You would just need to make sure that the note lasts for the length of the measure.

Quick Exercise: Set your metronome to one beat per second and again, hold down any key you like. Hold it down for the count of four clicks and then move on to play the next note.

Putting It All Together

Now that you know how the count works, and know how long to hold the keys down for and what the basic note values are, you can start playing around a little and we can move onto the more complex notes.

Again, if you were only to stick to full, half and quarter notes, there would only be so much variation that you would be able to achieve. You can divide it up even more to fit in more notes per measure and increase the tempo.

You don't actually change the speed, but you are holding the notes down for smaller periods at a time. It may take some getting used to so, if you are battling, to keep up, slow things down a bit by slowing the speed of your playing. As you get more used to this rate, and more familiar with the eighth notes, and sixteenth notes, you can start to speed up again.

Eighth Notes

Eighth notes are also known as quavers. This is like your pizza into eight pieces. To eat a piece won't take as long as it would if you were eating half the pizza because you are getting much less pizza. By the same token, you just need to hold the note down for a lot less time, and move faster through the notes in the same measure. Instead of fitting 4-beats into a measure, you need to fit in eight so you will need to speed up your metronome. The symbol for an eighth note is:

If there are two or more of these notes, the flag changes to a solid beam and connects the notes. This helps in making the beat a lot more obvious. It will look something like this:

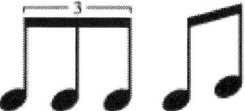

Sixteenth Notes

Sixteenth notes are also known as semi-quavers. The same rule applies to sixteenth notes. Like with eighth notes, when they are by single notes, they are shown with flags – except this time there are two flags.

When there are more than one of these in a row, the flags are changed to beams, as follows:

It is quite common to see four such notes placed together in this way because that represents one beat. You might also find it joined with an eighth note as follows:

Now, if you can slow things down a lot, it is pretty easy to play these notes. However, if you play them at the tempo that they are meant to be played at, it starts getting more complicated. That said, with practice, you will be fine to play these notes as well.

And dividing up the beat doesn't stop at sixteenths, some composers go a step further and halve it again so that it is 32nds, 64ths or 128ths. They show this in the composition by increasing the number of flags. I am not going to go into examples here because these are not as common as the eighth notes and sixteenth notes and should be left until you have had a bit more practice.

Rests

No matter how much practice you have, there is only a certain amount that you will be able to do. Your fingers are going to need a break from time to time and so will your audience. These breaks can be quick or a little longer, but the defining character of them is that you are not playing anything. You continue to count the beat, but you don't actually play or hold any kind of note.

In orchestral compositions, this will often be where the strings take over or someone playing another instrument gets their own solo. All you need to do is to relax your hands and keep them poised over the keys and make sure that you keep up with the count. Just like there are different note lengths, there are different rest periods. Let's have a look at these.

Whole And Half Rests

Let's say that you are playing a whole "C". You press the key and keep it depressed for a count of four beats. When you are playing half note, you keep it down for half as long. Rests will work in a similar fashion – you won't play anymore for the same number of beats.

I like to think of the symbol for the whole rest as a comfortable bed that you can sink into. You would relax for a decent period. It will always be on the fourth line or above so that it is easier to spot. It looks like this:

▃

The half rest is the same symbol, turned upside down. So, still a bed but a little less comfortable. It will always sit on the middle line. It looks like this:

▀

Quarter Rests and Beyond

These are the same as your quarter, eighth and sixteenth notes in terms of timing. Here are the symbols – from left to right, these are the symbols for the quarter, eighth and sixteenth rest respectively.

Time Signatures

In music, a time signature is what you use to find out the meter of the piece. The time signature is split into two numbers; the top number number tells you the meter of the piece you're playing. So, if the number is 4 over 4, that means there are four quarter note beats. If it is 2 over 2, there are two half note beats.

If the composer wants to use more than one type of note, like one-half note and two-quarter notes, that is fine – they could show this as 2 over 4 and 1 over 2. They do need to ensure that the top number adds up to a whole number in the end. So, one-half note and two-quarter notes, if we add them mathematically, would total 4 quarters in total and this makes sense.

If the composer tried to say three-quarter notes and one-half note, you would end up with too many beats, and this would not work. So, you should never see a time signature that is something like 5 over 4.

Common Time

Most composers stick to common time, i.e., 4 over 4. They indicate this by using the letter "C" in place of the standard time signature. It will appear directly after the clef symbol of the stave. This is how this would be displayed within the stave:

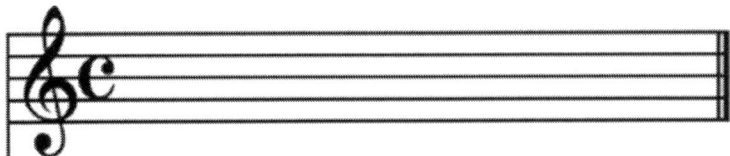

Chapter Summary

- The beat needs to be measured and kept at a steady pace.
- The faster the tempo that the notes are played at, the more energetic the pace of the piece.
- Beats are grouped in measures. These break up the music into equal sections. The composer will decide how many beats to use per measure.

- A whole note will take up a full measure, or four full beats. So, you would hold the note for the full length of that measure and only press the note once during that particular measure.
- A half note is half as long so there will be two beats in one measure.
- The notes can be divided into quarters, eighths and sixteenths as well. Each of these is shorter than the last so there will be more notes to play within each measure. This means that as the tempo increases the smaller the notes get.
- If you are still learning, slow down the tempo until you get used to playing the notes in the right succession. Then you can start worrying about speeding up again.
- The stems of the notes are arbitrary, used more as a way of differentiating the notes than having a very specific meaning.
- Rests are just as important when it comes to playing – they give you time to have a break and also give your audience a little break as well.
- A rest is usually similar in length to the note preceding it. The main thing to remember is to keep track of the beat.
- During a rest, keep your hands relaxed but poised at the ready for the next lot of notes.

Final Words

Well done – you have completed the program. Learning to play the piano can be fun, and it really is not that hard once you know the basics. It's a simple seven-step process:

- Step One: Learn the Keyboard and the keys.
- Step Two: Learn how and when to use the pedals.
- Step Three: Learn something about reading sheet music.
- Step Four: Practice your scales.
- Step Five: Learn about adding chords.
- Step Six: Learn when to use sharps and flats.
- Step Seven: Learn to get the tempo right.

In this book, we have started you off on the basics you need to play your first full composition. You should now be able to play some simple tunes and impress your friends with how fast your learned this skill.

From now forward, all it takes to really master the piano is to practice, and you get to decide how far you want to go. You can choose to practice every day, or trot your skills out on high days and holidays – it really is completely up to you.

Image Credit: Shutterstock.com

Printed in Poland
by Amazon Fulfillment
Poland Sp. z o.o., Wrocław